Launching
Your
First
Principalship

We dedicate this book to all principals: PAST, PRESENT AND FUTURE.

Launching Your First Principalship

A Guide for Beginning Principals

Barbara L. Brock
Marilyn L. Grady

CORWIN PRESS
A Sage Publications Company
Thousand Oaks, California

For information:

 Corwin Press
A Sage Publications Company
2455 Teller Road
Thousand Oaks, California 91320
www.corwinpress.com

Sage Publications Ltd.
6 Bonhill Street
London EC2A 4PU
United Kingdom

Sage Publications India Pvt. Ltd.
B-42, Panchsheel Enclave
Post Box 4109
New Delhi 110 017 India

Printed in the United States of America

Library of Congress Cataloging-in-Publication Data

Brock, Barbara L.
Launching your first principalship: A guide for beginning principals/Barbara L. Brock, Marilyn L. Grady.
    p. cm.
Includes bibliographical references and index.
ISBN 0–7619–4622–5—ISBN 0–7619–4623–3 (pbk.)
    1. First year school principals—United States—Handbooks, manuals, etc.
2. School management and organization—United States—Handbooks,
manuals, etc. I. Grady, Marilyn L. II. Title.
LB2831.93.B76 2004
371.2′012—dc21

                                                    2003010860

05   06   10   9   8   7   6   5   4   3   2

Acquisitions Editor:	Robert D. Clouse
Editorial Assistant:	Jingle Vea
Production Editor:	Melanie Birdsall
Copy Editor:	Elizabeth Budd
Typesetter:	C&M Digitals (P) Ltd.
Proofreader:	Tricia Toney
Indexer:	Julie Grayson
Cover Designer:	Michael Dubowe
Production Artist:	Lisa Miller

Contents

Introduction

You reached your goal. You have a principalship. Even though you dreamed of this day and worked hard to reach this goal, your excitement may be tinged with anxiety.

If you are feeling uncomfortable, keep in mind that you have a lot of company. The feelings and concerns that you are experiencing are common to most beginning principals. Culture shock and anxiety are normal when people move out of their comfort level into a new role and unfamiliar territory.

The book you are reading is designed to act as your paperback mentor. *Launching Your First Principalship* is written as a practical guide for aspiring and beginning principals. Veteran principals, experiencing a new situation, may find enrichment as well. The book addresses topics, such as the critical first days, tips for getting acquainted, ending and beginning the school year, communication skills, maximizing staff potential, solving problems and settling grievances, making changes, time management, and taking care of yourself. Interviews with first-year principals and seasoned veterans provide insights on common pitfalls to avoid and critical skills to acquire.

Although the primary purpose of the book is to serve as a paperback mentor for beginning principals, professors of educational administration and central office personnel will find the information useful in preservice preparation and beginning assistance programs.

Acknowledgments

Special thanks to the principals who shared their experiences and insights with us. Their perspectives inform our writing and challenge us to "get it right." Lynn Schneiderman's research assistance and Phyllis Hasse's manuscript preparation skills are gratefully acknowledged. We are always thankful for our families, their continued support, and generous patience. To the reviewers who took the time to carefully review the manuscript, we are especially appreciative.

Corwin Press gratefully acknowledges the contributions of the following reviewers:

Pablo Clausell
Superintendent of Schools
Perth Amboy Public Schools
Pert Amboy, NJ

Mike Parnell
Principal
Carrollton High School
Carrollton, MO

Charles Richards
Principal
Concord West Side Elementary School
Elkhart, IN

Judy Smith
Principal, Coach/Mentor
Southern California Comprehensive
Assistance Center
Los Angeles County Office of Education
Los Angeles, CA

Julie B. Boyd
Principal
Ashburn Elementary School
Ashburn, VA

Denny R. Vincent
Principal
Muhlenberg North High School
Greenville, KY

Nancy M. Moga
Principal
Callaghan Elementary School
Covington, VA

Rena Richtig
Professor
Department of Educational Administration
and Community Leadership
Central Michigan University
Mt. Pleasant, MI

Steve Hegner
Principal
Brady Middle School
Pepper Pike, OH

About the Authors

Barbara L. Brock, EdD, is Associate Professor of Education Department at Creighton University, Omaha, Nebraska. Her research interests include public and nonpublic education, specifically the principalship, leadership succession, and teacher development. She is coauthor, with Marilyn L. Grady, of *Rekindling the Flame: Principals Combating Teacher Burnout; From First Year to First Rate: Principals Guiding Beginning Teachers;* and *Principals in Transition: Tips for Surviving Succession.* In addition, she has written for a number of journals, including the *Journal of School Leadership, Connections, Educational Considerations, Clearinghouse, Catholic Education: A Journal of Inquiry and Practice, Momentum,* and the *Journal of Mid-Western Research Association.* She has been a teacher and administrator in K–12 schools as well as at the college level. She received her bachelor's degree in art education from Briar Cliff College, Sioux City, Iowa; her master's degree in education with a specialty in school administration from Creighton University; and her doctoral degree in administration, curriculum, and instruction from the University of Nebraska, Lincoln.

Marilyn L. Grady, PhD, is Professor of Educational Administration at the University of Nebraska, Lincoln. Her research areas include leadership, the principalship, and superintendent–board relations. She has more than 150 publications to her credit. She is the author or coauthor of 12 books. Her editorial board service includes *Educational Administration Quarterly, The Rural Educator, The Journal of At-Risk Issues,* the *Journal of School Leadership, Advancing Women in Leadership (On-Line Journal),* and the *Journal for a Just and Caring Education.*

She coordinates an annual conference on women in educational leadership that attracts national attendance and is in its fifteenth year. She has served on the executive board on the National Council of Professors of Educational Administration, the Center for the Study of Small/Rural Schools, and Phi Delta Kappa Chapter 15. She is a member of the American Educational Research Association, the International Academy of Educational Leaders, the National Rural Education Association, the National Council of Professors of Educational Administration, Phi Delta Kappa, and the Horace Mann League. She has been an administrator in K–12 schools as well as at the college and university level. She received her bachelor's degree in history from Saint Mary's College, Notre Dame, Indiana, and her PhD in educational administration with a specialty in leadership from The Ohio State University.

1 You've Got the Job

There are many ways to be a principal, but you have to find the way that best suits you.

—A beginning middle school principal

Congratulations and welcome to the principalship! You are about to embark on an exciting, challenging, and rewarding career. By now the thrill of your appointment has undoubtedly been replaced by a touch of anxiety—possibly sheer terror at the enormity of the responsibilities ahead. Progressing from the position of classroom teacher to the position of leader of an entire school is daunting. Most beginning principals experience a mix of emotions. A middle school principal explained, "I was nervous, anxious, scared, and overwhelmed, but also excited and enthusiastic."

You may be having doubts about your ability to handle the new job. One principal acknowledged, "knowing that any mistake I make would affect so many people was unnerving." Remember, you did not become principal by accident. You spent years studying and preparing for the position. Someone believed you were qualified. Someone has confidence in your ability to lead. Trust in yourself.

This chapter guides you through the concerns and issues that beginning principals experience, such as job anxiety, role change, leadership style, personal change, and relationship changes.

EMBRACE THE ROLE

The principal's role may have looked easy when you were a teacher or assistant principal. Now you find yourself awed at the magnitude of the job and wondering, "Where do I begin? One principal recalled, "It was the first day of school and I knew that the principal should visit classrooms to provide a calming, reassuring presence. But the thought that my presence—I, who felt unsure of myself—commanded such power was unnerving."

As a teacher or assistant principal, you knew exactly how to behave, but your role has changed now. Those comfortable behaviors that served you well in your previous role need to be modified or replaced. Your new role involves developing and leading adults, although from time to time modeling classroom teaching skills will be important. One elementary principal explained, "It felt strange not being responsible for teaching kids. I was in such a different role—smiling and greeting rather than orienting kids in school procedures for the year." An assistant principal recalled, "I was accustomed to following the principal's lead. Now I had all the responsibilities. For the first time I understood what the principal meant by 'the big picture.'"

Clarify Roles, Expectations, and Responsibilities

Before you begin, be certain that you have a clear understanding of what is expected of you. The responsibilities of a principal tend to mushroom in number and ambiguity. One elementary principal lamented, "I was surprised to find that my role included examining students for head lice, planning for asbestos removal, and searching trash cans for lost retainers." Another said, "According to the first graders, my job is to 'talk on the phone, dispense birthday treats, open milk cartons, and put lost teeth in envelopes to take home for the tooth fairy.'"

Although sometimes humorous, role conflict and ambiguity become major causes of stress and burnout for principals. It is imperative for beginning principals to clarify the roles, responsibilities, and expectations of their position. Following are measures you should take:

1. Read your job description and contract carefully.

2. Clarify specific responsibilities with your supervisor.

3. Identify the processes and criteria for your evaluation.

4. Establish two-way communication with your supervisor.

5. Determine how your role supports the goals of the school district.

6. Identify the expectations of constituent groups of the school: staff, parents, students, and community.

7. Identify conflicting expectations held by (a) your supervisor, (b) staff, (c) parents, (d) students, and (e) the community.

8. Search for compatible solutions to role conflicts.

WHAT KIND OF LEADER WILL YOU BE?

You may find it helpful to review the following leadership behaviors that you learned in your preparation program. They may take on new meaning now that you will be using them in a real principalship.

- Find a leadership model
- Look like a leader
- Make good decisions
- Interact with people
- Share information
- Know who you are
- Lead with your strengths
- Know what you stand for
- Act with deliberation
- Be a visionary leader
- Assume a calm, confident demeanor
- Be proactive
- Remain focused
- Get out of your office
- Act with integrity, ethics, and fairness
- Clarify roles and responsibilities

Find a Leadership Model

Begin by deciding what kind of leader you would like to become and by practicing those behaviors. One beginning principal suggested finding "a leadership style that's based on your strengths." You probably worked for and learned from principals whose behavior you admired and worked for other principals whose behavior you did not admire. Make a list of the traits and behaviors that you want to emulate and a second list of those traits and behaviors that you want to avoid. At the end of the year, examine these lists and evaluate behavior.

As you develop your list of desirable behaviors, keep in mind that leaders are:

- Honest
- Consistent
- Competent
- Dependable
- Fair
- Attentive
- Supportive
- Goal Oriented
- Trustworthy
- Energetic
- Visionary
- Innovative
- Communicators
- Organized
- Decision Makers

Look Like a Leader

An important step in gaining respect as a leader is looking like one. There are those who argue that it is not what is on the outside, but what is on the inside that counts. Whether you like it or not, people respond to appearances.

Presenting a professional image as a leader includes the following: a professional wardrobe, impeccable grooming, good posture, proper manners, and good conversational skills. Professional appearance as a teacher is different from professional appearance as a principal. One elementary principal said, "I hope my clothes look professional. The culture of my building is to look professional and dress attractively. Getting used to wearing suits has been difficult."

Make Good Decisions

An important part of your job is making decisions and choices for the school. For instance, assessing school needs and deciding if, when, and how changes should be made; allocating resources; negotiating conflicting demands; solving problems; and handling school crises are examples of decision-making opportunities (Straub, 2000).

Interact With People

The principalship is a people business. As leader of the school, you need to spend your time communicating, interacting, and collaborating with people, such as peers, parents, staff members, students, community members, supervisors, central office staff, and vendors.

You are also the symbolic figurehead of the school. You will be required to act as the school's spokesperson at meetings and perform a variety of ceremonial duties. For example, your presence is expected at student performances, athletic events, parent meetings, graduations, and award ceremonies. Plan on being asked to "say a few words" wherever you go.

Share Information

Your office is the hub of school information. You are the collector, keeper, and disseminator of information that emerges from the central office, school constituents, research, legislative updates, reports of best practices as well as grapevine news, gossip, gripes, and rumors.

You decide the importance and accuracy of information and determine which pieces of information should be shared with others. When information needs to be disseminated, you are the official spokesperson for the school.

Know Who You Are

Strong leadership requires self-knowledge, an educational philosophy, and professional goals. These attributes are identified through self-examination and reflection. Be able to articulate the following: What are my strengths? What are my weaknesses? Where do I want to be in my career ten years from now?

Lead With Your Strengths

Rely on your strengths, yet continue to improve your weaknesses. If your oral communication skills are limited, use as much written communication as possible until you have strengthened your oral communication skills.

Although personal strengths and weaknesses can be identified, in part, through self-appraisal, a thorough appraisal requires information and opinions from staff members, supervisors, and parents. A checklist to guide self-appraisal may be found in the resources (see Resource A).

Know What You Stand For

Indecisive individuals are buffeted by every whisper of opinion. As a leader, you must be able to articulate what you believe and what you value. Develop an educational platform, a written statement of your educational values. An educational platform provides a framework and perspective for choices and decisions and strengthens your resolve when confronted with problems. Leaders who know what they stand for are consistent in demonstrating and rewarding behaviors that support their beliefs. They are confident and ready to defend their ethical convictions. Individuals without convictions stand for nothing. Like puppets, their actions are driven by the convictions of others. A written guide for formulating an educational philosophy can be found in Resource B.

Act With Deliberation

From the beginning, know what kind of leader you want to be and how you want others to view you. Be consistent in demonstrating and rewarding behaviors that support school goals. Make your actions mirror your expectations.

Be a Visionary Leader

> *"Cheshire Puss . . . Would you tell me please, which way I ought to go . . . ?"*
> *"That depends a good deal on where you want to get to," said the Cat.*
> *"I don't much care where . . . so long as I get somewhere," said Alice.*

> *"Oh, you're sure to do that," said the Cat, "If you only walk long enough."*
>
> —Lewis Carroll, *Alice in Wonderland*

Like Alice, some principals react to events rather than having a vision that drives their decisions. They allow daily school activities to consume their time, becoming managers rather than visionary leaders.

Visionary leaders have a personal vision, believe that they can make a difference, and are driven to act on what they believe is possible. In collaboration with the school's stakeholders—teachers, staff, parents, students, and community members—they formulate a shared vision of what is desirable for the school. Members of the school community understand their role in achieving the collective vision for the school. Goals are formulated and action plans created.

Visionary leaders demonstrate five dominant qualities:

1. Visionary leaders are guided and motivated by personal values.

2. Visionary leaders have a commitment to the achievement of identified organizational goals.

3. Visionary leaders strive to develop a common sense of purpose and direction among all organizational members.

4. Visionary leaders are organizational innovators.

5. Visionary leaders consistently project, model, and attest to a future that represents something better. (Grady, 1990; Grady & LeSourd, 1990)

Assume a Calm, Confident Demeanor

> *Someone told me that I look like a principal. When I asked what that looked like, the woman said, "calm and not terribly talkative."*
>
> —An elementary principal

Successful principals exude auras of confidence and calm control. They listen more and talk less. They maintain their calm appearance even when things are in an uproar. By doing so, they instill confidence in their leadership and bring serenity to the school.

Be Proactive

Leaders plan ahead and anticipate issues that will arise. They forecast problems, anticipate needs and reactions, and consider consequences before taking action. When situations arise, they engage in "what if" thinking:

- What is on the horizon?
- If it happens, how will people react?
- Who will be affected?
- What will the consequences be?
- Should we take action?
- If we act, what should we do?
- What if we ignore the situation?
- Which consequences will occur?

Remain Focused

Leaders have a vision for the school and remain focused on their goals. Countless daily interruptions may be distracting, but they cannot deter leaders from their goals. Some principals keep their long-range goals taped to their desks. Others identify one goal and write it in their daily planners. They work to achieve the goal throughout the day, promptly returning to it after each distraction.

Get Out of Your Office

Effective leaders do not lead from behind their desks. They are visible, not only during times of crisis, grief, and celebration, but everyday— in the hallways, classrooms, cafeteria, and school grounds. They spend their time interacting with teachers, students, and parents. They know and are known by everyone; they know firsthand what is happening in the school.

Act With Integrity, Fairness, and Ethics

Leaders always do what is right, never what is simply expedient or easy. Treat everyone with respect. Remember your manners. Let courtesy be your guide.

EXPECT PERSONAL CHANGE

I lost weight, grew up, and developed thicker skin.
                                        —A beginning elementary principal

As you grow in leadership during your first year, your view of schools and education may change. Your work and interactions with people will mold and modify your attitudes and beliefs.

Profound leadership changes sometimes occur. Principals who begin their careers with democratic, collegial styles and a people orientation may become more bureaucratic, judgmental, directive, and task oriented. Since research indicates that administrators with democratic styles are more effective, this "transformation from Jekyll to Hyde" should be avoided (Schmidt, Kosmoski, & Pollack, 1998a, p. 12). Unfortunately, principals are often unaware that they have changed. What steps can you take to prevent unwanted change?

- Awareness
- Self-reflection
- Feedback from others
- Purposeful change

Awareness of the potential for change is the first step. Second, keep a journal and use it to reflect on your attitudes, decisions, and behaviors. Third, ask for feedback about your performance from supervisors and members of the school community. Rather than allowing undesirable habits to develop, make conscious choices about your behavior.

Sadness

A certain amount of nostalgia and sadness may be involved with change. Leaving the security and comfort of teaching can be difficult. One principal reported keeping boxes full of teaching materials for years—"just in case." Parting with the materials felt like "discarding part of myself." Another individual who assumed a principalship in the same school where she had taught said, "In retrospect, it wasn't a good idea, but I continued teaching one of my classes. I felt uncomfortable in the role of principal, so I clung to the comfortable security of teaching."

Loneliness

Many beginning principals are shocked at the loneliness of the job. Isolation stems from not being able to share information, discuss problems, or obtain feedback. Although staff can collaborate and assist in some decisions, many decisions belong solely to the principal.

Principals who work with assistant principals can create administrative teams within which issues, goals, and problems can be discussed. Other principals may discuss issues with secretaries, administrative assistants, and school counselors. Caution is necessary, however, because the principal supervises and evaluates these school employees. As one principal remarked, "My secretary was the best listener. However, regardless of what I said or suggested, she always replied, 'That's a good idea.'"

Confidentiality is also an issue. Principals need to be cautious about sharing information; much school information cannot be shared.

Beginning principals are often shocked to discover how much personal information parents, staff members, and students share with them. Often principals would prefer not to receive personal information that is unrelated to school issues. Personal information is confidential. A retired principal reflected, "I was told many secrets over the years, and I still keep them today." If, however, a student is being mistreated, is suicidal, or if any criminal activity is involved, that information must be given to appropriate authorities.

EXPECT RELATIONSHIPS TO CHANGE

> *My relationships changed from being a colleague to being a boss. It was an adjustment that took some time getting used to.*
> —A secondary principal

Once you assume a principal's position, relationships change. The emotional and social changes that accompany the role change from teacher or assistant principal to principal are complex. Although you may feel the same, others view you differently. Redefining your role is not a skill taught in graduate school. The process does not occur quickly or easily.

Loss of Camaraderie

The camaraderie, once enjoyed as a teacher, is absent and missed in the principal's role. Teachers are unaware of the conflicting demands, long hours, and pressures of being a principal. Teachers are not privy to all of the information used in decision making. It is a given that decisions will never please everyone. Unpopular duties must be assigned, and occasionally unfavorable personnel decisions must be made.

The principal is no longer part of the teachers' peer group. A surprised elementary principal who "thought everything would be the same" described teachers' responses as "a bit standoffish." Chilly greetings, complaints, and hushed voices are a harsh reality for beginning principals who once shared in the warmth of faculty camaraderie. Some beginning principals are shocked and dismayed when they discover that when they enter the faculty room, conversation stops. One principal remarked, "I was hurt when one of my friends, upon learning of my appointment as a principal, said, 'You've joined the enemy now.'" Even though faculty and staff members are friendly, the principal remains "the boss"—the person who has the power to make decisions that affect their work lives. One elementary principal commented, "It surprised me that people would say things like, 'It sure will be great working for you.' I always think of myself as working *with* people. It felt strange when people asked me if they could leave early . . . requests you make of a boss."

Changed Friendships

Friendships with former friends may be altered; some may disappear. Teachers who were once peers are now subordinates. Although most principals socialize and enjoy friendly interactions and relationships with their teachers, principals are not members of faculty social networks. Old friends may distance themselves.

A teacher who became principal in the school where she taught said, "I was shocked and hurt at how my former colleagues treated me. I expected their support. Instead, they responded with jealousy and distrust. I gained a new position and lost my friends." Another principal was told, "You joined the other side." An elementary principal was warned, "'We expect you to be our voice. Don't ever forget where you came from." Although it is possible for principals and teachers to maintain their friendships, the friendships may have a greater likelihood of survival when the new principal is in a different school.

If you have assumed leadership of a school where you previously taught, your relations with former colleagues will be different. You are now the boss, the person who makes decisions, supervises, and evaluates. One principal explained, "Because I had previously taught at the school, a staff member told me that he worried my former teammates would receive more favorable treatment." Another said, "Building new relationships with the teachers was a challenge. People see you differently and treat you differently when you're the boss, even though you don't feel different." Some friendships will disappear. Those that survive will be altered by the new work relationship.

Finding Support

My best friends are fellow principals. I'm part of a group that meets regularly to discuss mutual challenges, celebrate successes, and socialize. Sometimes we meet for dinner and include our spouses

—A veteran principal

Friendship and support can be found with your new peer group of principals. Meet them and organize study or social groups; join professional organizations; build a support community.

Your secretary can also become a member of your support group. Cultivating a close relationship with your secretary is essential. A loyal secretary is the protector of your privacy and time, a source of information, and a cheerleader when you are discouraged. A disloyal secretary, or one who inappropriately shares confidential information, is a dangerous and destructive foe who should be replaced.

One principal explained about her secretary,

> She knew everybody in the community. I always sought information from her before meeting with parents. Her pivotal position in the school put her in touch with teachers and parents, providing opportunities to hear their levels of satisfaction—things they liked and didn't like. She was a good sounding board for how the people might respond. Whenever I was discouraged and started bemoaning a project that failed, my secretary began her litany of my accomplishments in the school. She provided a wider perspective on a temporary setback and lifted my spirits. I treasured her loyalty and support.

Some principals confide in school counselors. Faculty members and parents may speak more candidly with the school counselor than with the principal. Counselors can provide alternative perspectives on a range of issues (Brock & Ponec, 1998; Ponec & Brock, 2000). One principal remarked, "I often used my school counselor as a sounding board before I presented a change to the faculty. She had a good sense of how the teachers would respond and often advised me of alternative methods of presenting ideas and change to them." Another said, "When I am having difficulty dealing with an individual, I often seek out ideas from the counselor" (Brock & Ponec, 1998).

Remember, however, that whether it is a secretary or a school counselor, you, as principal, are responsible for evaluating these individuals. Although secretaries and counselors can provide information and suggestions from alternate perspectives, a better choice for sharing administrative problems is another principal or a former professor with recent experience as a building principal.

HANG ON!

Do not give up at the first crisis. When the first school crisis occurs, many new principals yearn to be back in the classrooms. Some eventually give up and return to teaching. Others pursue central office positions or college teaching, erroneously thinking that these positions are less stressful.

Retreating in the first year or two is not the best choice. Discomfort in a new situation is normal. Feeling comfortable and confident in a new job takes about three years. Although you may be quaking inside, assume an air of confidence. One principal shared the advice her father gave her, "Look 'em in the eye and act like you know what you're doing. By the time they figure it out, you'll be an expert."

THE PRINCIPAL'S KEY

The first days and weeks can be overwhelming. According to a middle school principal, "I was really surprised at the number of hours that I needed to work in order to feel competent and on top of things. When I was a teacher I could plan my day and do what I planned. When you are an administrator, your time is not your own. It belongs to everyone else." An elementary principal reported being "shocked by the amount of energy required to perform the job."

Additionally, your carefully planned decisions are bound to disappoint someone. The principalship, however, is not a popularity contest, and a placid environment may signal a stagnant environment. According to one veteran principal, "As long as people debate what you're doing, you know you've got them thinking."

Many beginning principals long for the security of their classrooms where they felt confident and capable. One beginning principal reported, "I went home every night and cried, frustrated and furious at myself for leaving teaching. " Added to the frustration is the loneliness for friends and the camaraderie experienced as a teacher.

Frustrated and lonely, many beginning principals are tempted to quit during their first year. A better choice is to take adequate time to adjust to the newness of the role as well as the setting. Similar to beginning teachers, beginning principals require time to become acclimated to their new role.

> *My first year as principal was similar to being a first-year teacher. Everything was new and somewhat confusing. But by the second year, I loved being a principal. There's nothing like the thrill of seeing the school improve and students succeed because of your ideas and initiative.*
>
> —A third-year principal

2 Get Acquainted

The People, the Place, the Culture

You can't command respect; you have to earn it. And everyone is watching everything you do

—A beginning middle school principal

Your job as principal begins the minute you sign the contract. Gradual orientation to the position is rare. Most new principals are greeted with a deluge of mail, messages, and meeting requests. As soon as possible, become acquainted with the office staff, school personnel, parents, students, the building layout, and the basic procedures for operating the school. Remain objective until you have had time to meet everyone and to examine the entire organization. Once you have acquainted yourself with the people, the place, and the culture, you can move ahead with confidence!

THE PEOPLE

Each school serves an internal public composed of students and staff and an external public that consists of parents and members of the community. Meeting the people in each of these groups should be a priority. Most people will be welcoming and anxious to meet you. You may initially meet skepticism, distrust, and opposition from a few, however. Some people react negatively when confronted with change, so do not take negative responses personally. Talk to as many people as possible and listen carefully for their expectations.

Identify Expectations

The expectations of the school's reference groups, namely, teachers and staff, parents, students, and community members, help determine the roles of the principal. Each group has a set of expectations based on their perspective and needs.

• Teachers and staff expect the principal to be an instructional leader, to keep the school running efficiently, to communicate well, to be a visible presence in the building, to be a good disciplinarian, to involve teachers in school decisions, and to be supportive. The order in which they prioritize expectations and the preferred method of delivery varies.

• Parents base their expectations on their own school experiences, past interactions with principals, and the strengths and weaknesses of the school. The more heterogeneous the community, the more diverse their expectations will be.

• Students have expectations related to the role of the principal in their school experience. Be sure to gather their opinions. After all, they are the reason the school exists.

• Community members exercise power through their local school board that establishes policies and approves expenditures. Gathering information about the community's attitude toward the school will be valuable information as you initiate changes.

Last, but very important, are the expectations of your superiors. They probably expressed a set of expectations when you were hired. Meeting these expectations will likely determine your retention. Consequently, clarifying which administrative responsibilities you are required to handle is vital. Establish an ongoing dialogue and obtain periodic feedback from your immediate supervisor.

Compatibility of Expectations

The school's publics, or reference groups, generally support principals who meet their expectations. If, however, expectations of one or more groups are not compatible, the principal must convince group members to modify their expectations. Principals who do not meet expectations of a particular group lose that group's support, and conflict erupts.

The first step in gaining support is getting acquainted, identifying expectations, and establishing trust.

GET ACQUAINTED

The first days are critical to long-term success. All eyes are on you. Teachers, students, and parents are watching what you do and listening to what you say. Making a good first impression is critical as first impressions are formed quickly and tend to linger. Changing first impressions is extremely difficult. Although there are no magic formulas to ensure a successful beginning, the following strategies have been helpful to other successful principals.

Meet the people. Smile, ask questions, observe, listen, and learn. Listen, not only to what people say, but how they say it. Listen to their emotions. Pay attention to what they do not say. Although most beginning principals admit, "Remembering all the names and faces is tough," doing so as quickly as possible is essential.

Avoid Hasty Promises

Since many individuals will be anxious to meet you, you will have many visitors. Although most will welcome you, some will bear personal agendas or grudges. They come seeking favors or alliances. Listen carefully and take notes. Make no promises, however, even though requests may look simple and clear-cut. You do not know all the facts, implications, or historical baggage that may be involved in seemingly simple requests. One beginning principal reported learning a lesson "that cost her district a considerable amount of money" when she "allowed herself to be swayed" by a persuasive teacher.

When people make requests, record their names and the request and promise that you will look into the situation. Be certain to contact them with a decision once you have thoroughly familiarized yourself with the issue.

Some visitors will bear tales about your predecessor. Rather than encouraging the recitation of your predecessor's transgressions, focus the conversation on the person who has come to visit you. What is it that they want or need? What action do they want you to take? Remain objective, make no promises, and speak positively about your predecessor and the school. One beginning principal remarked, "I just smiled and kept my mouth shut. I let people know that that chapter was closed, and we were moving on to the next." Remember, you do not know the whole story yet.

Keep a list of all visitors, noting dates and conversation topics. As the weeks progress, you may discover relationships between people, issues, and requests. Themes will emerge that provide glimpses of problems to be resolved or barriers to circumvent.

Make Friends With the Office Staff

Make friends with the office staff. Take them to lunch. Let them know how much you appreciate their assistance. An elementary principal observed, "My first week began when all the office staff was off on vacation. Looking back, I made a huge mistake by not meeting with them before they left for vacation." Another principal recalled a happier experience:

> I took the office staff to lunch during my first week on the job. The staff selected a nearby restaurant that was unfamiliar to me. I got lost and drove around aimlessly until I spotted them standing in the middle of the street—flagging me down. I took a lot of ribbing about failing my first "leadership task," but the event paved the way for a relaxed and congenial relationship.

Make the Custodian Your Ally

A good working relationship with the building's custodians is essential to a peaceful and productive school year. Most principals note that the school's caretakers can make life pleasant or enormously miserable. One principal recalled an unfortunate beginning with a happy ending:

> My first day on the job, a man, who I assumed was the custodian, burst into my office and announced that he was shutting off the water for a few hours. I introduced myself and asked his name. He pointed to his chest and snarled, "Name's on the shirt. Didn't like any of the other principals. Probably won't like you."
>
> A few days later I arrived to find my office in a shambles. Ladders blocked the entrance and my desk was covered with stacked chairs, wastebaskets, and tools. The blinds were off the windows, lying on top of the conference table. When I voiced my dismay, he explained, "You complained that the blinds were broken, so I'm fixing them. Don't know how long it will take."
>
> I wondered if I would ever win him over. However, my patience paid off when several months later, he burst in again and announced, "You're going to be OK. First principal I've liked."

Wise principals seek opportunities to establish amiable relationships and make the custodian part of the school team. One principal revealed her strategy:

> I made sure that the custodian understood he was an important member of the school team. When I hired him I introduced him to students and teachers and enlisted their assistance in helping him keep our school clean. I invited him to school functions, kept him informed of school issues, and listened to his concerns. Years later he told me that he enjoyed his work because he felt like he was contributing to the education of the students.

Match Names and Faces

Learn as much as you can about the staff, students, and families before school opens. Study photos of staff members and memorize their names and assignments. Match personnel files and evaluations with the faces.

Learn the names of the school's families and match them with photos of their children. Once school begins, you need to learn the names of students as quickly as possible. Devise a plan, such as learning the names of students in a classroom or a grade level, each week. It is useful when the names of elementary students are taped on the fronts of their desks. One principal reported, "I get acquainted with students by being in classrooms every day, greeting students in the morning, and being at the exit door when they leave. If I don't know their names, I ask. I try to be *visible*."

Meet the Teachers

> *I asked staff to fill out a short "all about me questionnaire." I learned the names of their spouses and children and made a point of asking about them.*
>
> —A high school principal

Because teachers' work satisfaction is closely tied to their communication with the principal, you will need to make frequent conversations with teachers a priority (Brock & Grady, 2000). One principal noted, "I think people want to be noticed; so, I try to stop and talk to people and be less on a mission."

Invite each of the teachers to meet with you to get acquainted; and then, continue the practice regularly throughout the year. Meet with small groups that share common interests or concerns. Inquire about levels of satisfaction, problems, needs for assistance, and perceptions of school strengths, weaknesses, and future needs. Rooney (1998) suggested asking two questions: "What about the school do you truly value and want to retain at all costs? What in the school needs to be discarded?" (p. 78).

Teachers want to know the principal's educational philosophy, beliefs about students, expectations, and plans for faculty interaction. Share your philosophy, beliefs, and goals for the year. Invite questions. Identify teachers who wield power with the faculty. Enlist their support. The time spent with teachers developing rapport will reap many dividends.

One elementary principal reflected on the need for personalized communication,

> I was perplexed when a group of teachers said they were unhappy and requested that I meet with them. They sought reassurance regarding my satisfaction with their classroom management. They were worried about potential curriculum changes. I thought I had communicated that information in faculty meetings. However, my generalized comments failed to address their specific concerns. Consequently, they distrusted my motives and intentions.

Include the Auxiliary Staff

Noncertified staff members are a vital but often overlooked segment of the school community. Get acquainted with the cafeteria workers, bus drivers, paraprofessionals, school nurse, and other auxiliary staff members. Establishing harmonious relationships with the noncertified personnel is essential to maintaining an effective school.

Meet the Parents

A change in school leadership creates tension for parents. You are a stranger who will directly impact their child's education. How will the school operate under your leadership? What changes will you make?

Securing parents' trust takes time. One veteran principal recalled, "After I left, parents continued to call me at my new school. They wanted to verify the appropriateness of decisions made by the new principal. I was shocked." Getting to know parents personally is key to establishing trust. Principals suggested activities such as, "inviting small groups of parents for coffee, conversation and donuts, . . . hosting 'ice cream socials,' and seizing every opportunity to meet parents individually." First and foremost, parents need to believe that the principal cares about the students.

Remember Volunteers and Student Teachers

Volunteers and student teachers have privileged knowledge of the daily functioning of the school. You will want to meet these individuals, understand their roles, determine their levels of satisfaction, and establish a dialogue with them.

Students

Seize opportunities to speak with students. Regardless of age, they have opinions, and they want and deserve your personal attention. After all, serving them is the reason the school exists. A retired principal related an important lesson:

> I was in a department store when a sales associate rushed over and announced, "I know you. You were my principal when I was in first grade!" I asked how she recognized me so many years later. She explained, "You used to invite us to your office to visit you and I thought that was the greatest thing."

Change Brings Anxiety

During your initial meetings, you will notice tension. Changes in leadership produce some level of anxiety for everyone in the school community. People fear the unknown. They fear loss of autonomy, territory, resources, and relationships. Although some people will be delighted about a change in leadership, others will be unhappy. A few people may resent your presence. Individuals loyal to your predecessor may attempt to sabotage your efforts by withholding critical information (Brock & Grady, 1995; Hart, 1993).

Examine Lingering Baggage

People's past experiences affect their responses to you. The ghosts of your predecessors may linger and haunt you. The duration and focus of this uneasiness varies according to the nature and depth of the past experiences. Manifestations of these responses include the following:

- Hostility
- Mourning
- Controversy
- Heroism
- Lack of acceptance
- Resentment

Hostility

Teachers and parents who have had unpleasant experiences with other principals may initially distrust you or display hostility toward you. As one new principal lamented, "They didn't give me a chance. The teachers were hostile before they even got to know me." Earning the trust of these individuals requires time and patience.

Mourning

A school community that has lost a beloved principal may resent your presence. The person they lost will be elevated in status, and nothing you do will quite "measure up" to previous standards. Be patient and understanding of the mourning that may linger throughout the year. One principal reported, "When I referred a student for special education or counseling, some parents called my predecessor to confirm that I had made an appropriate decision. They trusted him and wanted his reassurance. It took time and patience, but eventually I won them over and the parents began to trust me."

Controversy

If you succeed a principal who has been controversial or was terminated, two camps are likely: those who supported and those who did not support the principal. As a newcomer, the better choice is to not take sides in the controversy. Speak kindly of your predecessor when possible. When in doubt, say nothing. Keep people focused on the present.

Heroism

It may be easier to assume a principalship in a school that has suffered from poor leadership in the past. One principal explained, "If you succeed a principal who has been lax, the people will be anxious for change. You will be welcomed as the savior—the hero." If you have been welcomed as a hero, be prepared to face enormous challenges and a community that expects immediate solutions.

Lack of Acceptance

In a school where leadership changes have been frequent, the faculty may assume that you, too, are a "short-timer." They may be reluctant to accept your leadership or endorse any long-term changes that you propose. Additionally, the faculty may have assumed leadership tasks ordinarily handled by the principal, and they may be reluctant to relinquish those tasks. One principal reported,

> Initially, the teachers regarded me as temporary and looked toward faculty leaders rather than me for direction. They sabotaged my leadership by withholding vital information. Even the office staff dismissed my authority. The secretary advised, "If you want something from the files, tell me and I'll get it. Every principal who comes through here messes up the files."

Resentment

Beware! Some members of the faculty may have been candidates for the position you hold. Winning acceptance from them will be particularly challenging. Find out who they are, and include them on your leadership team. Acknowledge their skills and find outlets for their talents.

Examine the School's Context

An important piece of the information to gather is the school's history. Each school has a unique history that needs to be heard. Although your immediate concerns will likely be meeting the people and preparing for the school year, understanding the larger context of the school is equally important. Ideally, the school's history and demographics should be examined before accepting the principalship.

The history of a school can affect the relationship between the school and the community. New principals will want to know the following: (a) When was the school founded? (b) Did the school result from consolidation? (c) What have been the dominant school–community issues? Underlying historical factors may emerge when a school change is proposed (Brock & Grady, 1995). As one principal explained,

> I knew that my school resulted from a bitter consolidation struggle several years before I arrived on the scene. I failed to recognize how much bitterness simmered beneath the surface. As soon as I proposed major school changes, I experienced the reemergence of the two rival groups and major disagreements ensued.

Part of a school's history is its reputation in the community. School reputations are built on facts, misinformation, gossip, conjecture, and athletic prowess (Brock & Grady, 1995). Accurate or not, these perceptions are reality to community members.

Determine whether the school's reputation is based on accurate or inaccurate information. If the school's reputation is based on inaccurate information, talk with community members to correct the inaccuracies. Be proactive in presenting accurate information to the community. A school–community relations program that promotes two-way communication is essential.

The Community

Factors, such as the size of the population, ethnicity, age, and economics of a community affect interactions with the school. Principals should consider the following:

- What is the ratio of people with school-age children compared with those without school-age children?
- What ethnic groups are present in the community?
- How is the community changing?
- What is the unemployment rate in the community?
- What is the educational level of the community?

The differences that exist between the principal's background and the school and community are important, too. When the principal differs in race, ethnicity, culture, or socioeconomic background, assimilation and acceptance of the principal may be more difficult. An elementary principal said, "When I became principal of a school with a majority Caucasian population, parents informed me that because I was Black, I would never understand White children."

Residents of rural areas may be skeptical of principals from "the big city," just as city residents may question the abilities of a "rural" principal. A community accustomed to male principals may approach a female principal with concern and skepticism. A female middle school principal reported, "I received phone calls from parents, mostly fathers, warning me that I would never be able to handle teenage boys."

Principals who are aware of these differences may be able to minimize the differences and focus on shared concerns. Principals must be alert to the culture, norms, and beliefs of the school and community.

The Neighborhood

Becoming familiar with the neighborhood and larger community is also important. Drive around, walk around, and visit businesses in the area. Find out where the community gathers, gossips, shops, plays, and worships. See where the students live and where they "hang out" after school. Talk with business owners and listen to their views about the school. An elementary principal reported, "I hosted a series of neighborhood walks to meet families and students."

Consider the forms of transportation the students use, the routes they take to school, and the school's role in providing transportation. Notice traffic patterns, construction sites, and industrial areas that pose safety problems for students.

Community Leaders

Become acquainted with the community leaders—the power brokers in the community. You will want to gain their support and include them on your team. Join community organizations. Social and civic occasions present opportunities to tell the good news about the school.

Become a Master Schmoozer

Principals have many opportunities to mingle with the community. Although some principals view these gatherings as wastes of time, other principals capitalize on them.

Gatherings of people present opportunities to become acquainted, share ideas, and garner support. Politicians have schmoozed for decades. Small talk can be used to (a) break down barriers, (b) establish mutual respect, (c) share information and ideas, and (d) build support for the school.

Learn the art of meeting and greeting people. Suggestions include the following:

- Have a purpose in mind (meeting people, testing an idea, gaining support).
- Pause at the entrance to examine the room and decide where to begin.
- Enter smiling and confident.
- Try to speak to everyone in the room.
- Listen intently.
- Be sincere and honest.
- Prepare a 3-second message to convey to the people you meet.

Remember,

> *You can get by on charm for about 15 minutes, after that, you had better know something.*
> —Tom Hennessy

Schmoozing is useful when principals are sincere and their message is honest. Nothing breeds contempt and distrust more quickly than thinly disguised insincerity.

The Place

In addition to knowing the people, the principal needs to be well acquainted with the building. Embarrassing blunders can be avoided by taking time to get acquainted with the physical layout and operation of the school.

Learn the Building Layout

Investigate every nook and cranny of the building and grounds. Take along a notebook to jot down needed repairs, physical hazards, and security problems. Be sure you have keys for every door, and make sure you are able to unlock them.

Master the Mechanics

> One of the first critical tasks is learning to operate phones, security systems, intercoms . . .
>
> —A high school principal

Before school opens in the fall, learn how to operate the office machines, bell and alarm systems, telephones, technology, and locks. Ask your staff to teach you how to operate these systems. As one principal remarked, "It's difficult to demonstrate your leadership ability when you don't know which key unlocks the front door of the school."

Use these opportunities to become acquainted with your staff. If you are mechanically challenged, try using humor to survive the indignities of the mechanics. One principal reported the following:

> Some of my funniest experiences involved performing mechanical tasks, such as shutting down bells and using the phone system. One day the alarm system went off, and I couldn't shut it off. The kids were outside forever while I'm on the phone, siren blaring in my ear talking to the alarm company.

Learn Safety and Security Measures

Do a building and grounds walk carrying a copy of the plans for building evacuations, natural disasters and security. Locate fire alarms, fire extinguishers, evacuation routes, and building shelters. According to one principal, "Some of the most difficult problems I encountered were caused by my lack of familiarity with lights, alarms, and basic security measures in the building."

Read the school's crisis plan with the assumption that a crisis will occur. Plan how you will handle it.

Learn Policies and Procedures

> One of the most immediate needs is learning the school's and district's policies and procedures.
>
> —An elementary principal

Become familiar with procedures for student discipline, standardized testing, fundraisers, collecting money at school, field trips, student illness and injury, immunizations, attendance and tardiness, school assemblies, grading, emergency drills, athletic events, and lunches (Brock & Grady, 1995). One principal reported, "I struggle to answer people's questions when they call. At this point, I can seldom answer them . . . so I am developing reference lists to assist me." Another principal said, "When people ask questions or make requests and I don't have an answer, I admit it. I write down the question or request, find the answer, and get back to them."

Read the Documents

Familiarize yourself with the following documents: mission statement, school and district long-range goals, curriculum, school board policies, personnel roster, student rosters, school schedule, job descriptions, supervision and evaluation plans, the principal's job description, school handbooks, long-range maintenance plans, and previous school calendars. Review the school's standardized test scores to determine strengths and weaknesses. Review the policy for admitting and discharging students. Read the past school newsletters, faculty bulletins, and the minutes of the following: faculty meetings, parent–teacher organizations, student council, and school board (Brock & Grady, 1995). Resources C and D provide reminders of the information you should have collected before accepting the principalship. It may be helpful to review these areas so that you can acquire any information that may help ensure your success in the new principalship.

Examine the Finances

Learn the financial structure of the school and district. Read the school's budget and determine your financial responsibilities. If you are responsible for any bank accounts or petty cash, review past records and accounting procedures. An audit of past financial records may be in order.

School Culture

Tread Carefully

Last, but not least, become familiar with the school's culture. You are the newcomer to a school that is steeped in tradition and history. The behavioral patterns, traditions, values, core beliefs, and norms are part of the school's culture. These are powerful forces that shape and sustain the school system (King & Blumer, 2000).

Principals new to a school must be cautious about interfering with time-honored traditions and practices. This is "sacred ground" on which new principals should not tread. "Test the water" before making changes. Many a beginning principal has paid dearly for such transgressions. One high school principal explained,

> I made one small change to an annual school event. Instead of selecting a handful of students to conduct a ceremony, I included all of the school's students in some way. I thought parents would be pleased that more students would be participating. Obviously, I was wrong. I was bombarded with calls and visits from unhappy parents who informed me that my changes had destroyed a cherished school tradition.

Learn the Culture

Each school has its own particular culture. School inhabitants call it, "the way we do things here." Do your homework. Cultural understanding requires careful observing and listening. According to one principal, "Learning a school's culture is like searching for a buried treasure. People will assist you in your quest and share the stories and traditions of their culture, if you show interest, enthusiasm, and respect."

Understanding a school's culture requires patience, careful observation, and thoughtful insight.

1. Examine the school's physical surroundings, artistic displays, history, written documents, manner of employee dress, traditions, rituals, and ceremonies.

2. Listen to the school's stories, myths, and tales of heroes and heroines.

3. Observe how the staff greets visitors, welcomes parents, interacts with each other, and treats students.

4. Identify the values espoused in school publications.

5. Determine the underlying assumptions and values that permeate the school.

Cultural Detriments

Sometimes aspects of a school's culture may be detrimental to school goals and require change. Principals who hastily tread on prevailing culture increase their probability of failure, however. Cultural change requires complete knowledge of the prevailing, or descriptive culture; the vision, or prescriptive culture that the school system seeks; plus trust of school participants (King & Blumer, 2000).

Before considering changes that affect the school's culture, learn everything possible about the culture of the school and district. Visualize how to make things better. Listen for evidence of the prescriptive culture, the vision that the school system seeks to develop (King & Blumer, 2000). Although your task is to shape the school's descriptive culture into one that best serves the needs of the students, timing and trust are critical to successful change.

Establish Trust

Trust, although essential to a principal's success, is earned gradually. Principals earn trust by listening, sharing information, and showing respect for the people, community, and culture in which they work. Principals are viewed as trustworthy when they are perceived as genuine, fair, committed to the school, visible, and willing to listen and extend themselves beyond the school into the community (Davis, 1997).

The time you spend gathering information and getting acquainted are the initial steps in building trust.

THE PRINCIPAL'S KEY

The beginning principal must be prepared to examine all aspects of the school and community carefully, and to meet many people. The information and insight gained in the early days of the principalship is vital and must be acquired quickly. This information is the foundation for your years in the principalship. As you engage in the process of gaining information and meeting people, remember that this information is your personal "pot of gold," because knowledge is power.

3 Beginning and Ending Your School Year

Organization, planning, and follow-through are critical skills for a beginning principal.

—A third-year veteran

An orderly, efficient school environment is prerequisite to the emergence of visionary leadership and optimal student learning. Teachers and staff, parents, and community members want the principal to be a competent manager who monitors and directs the school's daily operations and overall environment. Carrying out that role means that the principal must be able to plan, organize, communicate, and carry out routine and unexpected events and activities that occur throughout a school year.

The principal must also establish and manage the recurring systems that keep the school running, such as calendars, schedules, meetings, ceremonies, procedures, inventories, budgets, and services. These systems provide a framework of stability and predictability within which the school operates.

At first, organizational tasks may seem overwhelming, especially the amount of planning required at the beginning and ending of a school year. Therefore, this chapter is designed to assist you in organizing the beginning and ending of your first school year. After the first year, the planning will become easier. One principal recalled, "I was so nervous my first year—always afraid that I was going to forget something or make a huge mistake. But the second time around, I knew what to do, and it felt pretty routine."

BEGINNING THE SCHOOL YEAR

Only a duck should wing it.

—Unknown

The Importance of Planning

Careful planning before the school year begins ensures calm opening days and establishes an orderly tone for the school year. Most principals plan for the academic year during the summer or between school terms or sessions, depending on the structure of the calendar year.

Assume Nothing

Beginning principals may find that some of the planning and tasks were completed by the previous principal. Nothing should be taken for granted, however. All plans and tasks should be reviewed. Remember, as the new principal, you are the person who is responsible.

Create a Checklist

Determining where and how to begin can be overwhelming. Many principals develop a checklist that is based on personnel titles or school tasks. Findley and Findley (1998, p. 57) suggested divisions according to:

- Faculty members
- Counselors
- Coaches
- Band and Vocal Music Directors
- Students
- Parents
- Custodians
- Food Service Workers
- Bus Drivers
- Office Operations
- Media services

Meeting with leaders of each of these divisions will assist you in understanding the work that needs to be accomplished. By considering each of these divisions, tasks can be divided into manageable units.

Although no list is adequate for all schools, a general list provides a starting point. Examining functions is another way to approach tasks. The most immediate issues to address include the following:

1. Finding out if all personnel have been contracted for the upcoming year. If openings exist, find out the district's process for recruiting and hiring. Become familiar with contracts and salary schedules.

2. Determining if any litigation is pending against the school. If so, contact the district's attorney and familiarize yourself with the situation.

3. Determining if a class schedule is in place for the coming year. Review previous schedules and consult with key teachers before designing one.

4. Preparing class lists.

5. Preparing duty rosters for faculty.

6. Developing an induction program for first-year teachers.

7. Reviewing school or district staff-development plans.

8. Preparing a welcome-back letter for faculty and staff that includes the dates, times, and agenda for the first faculty in-service day, staff meetings, and opening school activities.

9. Preparing a welcome-back letter for students and families.

10. Assigning students to teachers or homerooms. Review past practices and procedures before making decisions.

11. Determining whether students' addresses and records are updated. Find out if information has been received on incoming students. Discuss procedures with office staff.

12. Checking that student or family handbooks are current and ready for distribution.

13. Meeting with the contractors and architects if repairs or construction projects are underway. Make arrangements for building accommodations if construction is not completed when school opens.

14. Locating the summer schedule for cleaning and maintenance of the building and grounds. Check on progress.

15. Reviewing job descriptions of auxiliary personnel.

16. Preparing work schedules for auxiliary personnel.

17. Verifying that books, materials, and furnishings have been ordered.

18. Preparing and distributing the school calendar.

19. Determining the repair and replacement needs for electronic and media equipment.

20. Verifying that all required data or documentation from the previous year has been submitted to the school's governing bodies.

21. Reviewing the school's budget and previous financial records.

22. Determining the principal's responsibilities relative to student transportation.

23. Reviewing the school's security, weather, emergency, and crisis plans. Learn the procedures and how to operate warning devices.

The School Calendar

A task central to the organization of the school year is creation of the school calendar. A well-constructed school calendar is the pivot around which all activities rotate. As one high school principal testified, "I live by my calendar." All members of the school community use the calendar as a framework for personal and professional planning. Consequently, the entire school community depends on the accuracy of the calendar. Errors and changes cause confusion and frustration and undermine the principal's credibility.

According to one beginning principal, the possibility of error is worrisome, "I was paralyzed by the possibility of making an error . . . knowing that it would affect so many people." In spite of meticulous proofreading, mistakes can and will occur. The world will not end. If you discover an error after the calendar has been distributed, send an apology and correction to all recipients as quickly as possible. Minimize the possibility of error by reviewing previous calendars to identity regularly scheduled and annual events, activities, and ceremonies. Use office staff, teachers, and colleagues as additional sources of information. When the calendar is finished, have as many people as possible proofread it. Then proofread it again.

Be aware that some calendar items may be "untouchables." The state and district, as well as the school's traditions, are determining factors in the design of school calendars. The state and school district may require a specified number of calendar days, hours per day, staff development days, and holidays. The school's traditions may be linked to other events, ceremonies, and activities. These may be considered "sacred" and are best left unchanged during the first year of a principal's tenure. The wise beginning principal earns the trust and cooperation of key members of the school community before removing or altering any "sacred" school tradition.

Important Letters

As the new kid on the block everyone will be anxious to meet you. Send letters to returning staff, parents, and students expressing enthusiasm about joining the school and your interest in getting acquainted. Indicate times when you will be available and invite everyone for informal chats. Include a copy of the school calendar, information on the opening days of school, and faculty in-service days.

New students and families will appreciate a letter that welcomes them to the school and provides additional information on orientation and school programs. Parents with students in an entry-level grade in the school may experience heightened anxiety, be unfamiliar with school routines, and require more detailed information.

Members of the school community will scrutinize letters to determine something about your personality and leadership style. Since this is their first impression of you, careful wording and conscientious editing are essential. Tips for letter writing include the following:

1. Identify the purpose of the letter.

2. Consider the maturity, education, background, and interest level of the reader.

3. Write in a conversational tone, using short, clear precise words; avoid technical jargon and flowery language.

4. Get to the point; be brief.

5. Edit, edit, edit; have someone else proofread. Then proofread again.

New Teachers

New teachers and staff will appreciate a letter or phone call from you, especially if you were not part of their hiring process. Welcome them to the school and arrange to meet with each person.

The induction for new teachers should begin soon after they are hired. Begin with a tour of the school, an introduction to the office staff, and access to the classroom and teaching materials. Give teachers as much time as possible to become familiar with the curriculum and teaching materials.

If the new teachers are unfamiliar with the city, they may need assistance in locating housing, medical and financial services, day care, schools for their children, and possibly employment for a trailing spouse. Principals in larger districts should utilize whatever human resource or personnel services are available for new employees. In smaller districts, a staff member should be assigned to assist the newcomer with relocation issues.

The term "beginning teachers" describes a variety of individuals. Beginning teachers may be directly out of college, returning to the profession after an alternative venture, or starting a second career. Other teachers may be veteran teachers, yet new to your school. If your school district has an alternative certification program, the beginning teachers may lack preparation in pedagogy. Consequently, the content of the school's induction program must be tailored to fit individual needs.

Regardless of their circumstances, all beginning teachers undergo dramatic changes during their first year of teaching. How well they develop as teachers depends largely on the quality of the school's induction program and their ongoing professional support. The school's induction program should consist of the following:

- *Initial orientation:* An introduction to the district, the school, colleagues, and an explanation of their responsibilities.

- *A mentor program:* Training and assignment of skilled and experienced teachers to work with beginning teachers.

- *Teacher needs assessment:* Assessments to determine the needs of beginning teachers at intervals throughout the school year.

- *Ongoing, individualized assistance:* Assistance provided according to individualized needs of the beginning teacher.

- *Program evaluation:* A summative evaluation of the induction program based on multiple sources.

Additional information on developing a beginning teacher induction program may be found in *From First-Year to First-Rate: Principals Guiding Beginning Teachers* (Brock & Grady, 2001).

Faculty In-Service

Returning teachers look forward to the opening faculty days as a chance to (a) socialize and "catch up" with colleagues, (b) obtain class rosters and assignments, and (c) have time to work in their classrooms. Be sure to provide refreshments and time to socialize.

Since you are new, the teachers will be anxious to see you and hear what you have to say. Your welcoming remarks are extremely important. They provide a tone for relationships with faculty as well as identify expectations for the year. Faculty members will listen for your

1. Educational philosophy and expectations

2. Communication style

3. Praise for past efforts

4. Acknowledgment of the difficulty, yet importance, of their work

5. Encouragement and inspiration

6. Assurance that their ideas and experience are valued and that they will be included in decisions that affect them.

As one principal suggested,

It's important for teachers to establish close working relationships and to perceive themselves as part of a team. I encourage this by providing time for socialization and refreshments before the opening meeting. My introductory message identifies a theme for the year that relates to our mission statement. I try to make the opening day memorable and establish a unifying theme for the school year by presenting each teacher with a memento, such as a book bag, T-shirt, or pin bearing the theme.

The opening faculty gathering is a good time to

- Introduce new staff members and their mentors.
- Acknowledge any notable achievements of returning faculty members.
- Provide an update on summer happenings, new district or legal mandates, or notable enrollment changes.
- Review the crisis plan and key agents.
- Discuss a schedule and topics for the year's staff development plan.
- Review any changes in the student discipline code, supervision and evaluation plan, student or faculty handbooks, curriculum, disaster drills, student injury reports, attendance procedures, report card, or grading system.
- Distribute a packet containing schedules, class rosters, duty assignments, and student emergency contact cards.

Keep in mind that the teachers are interested in preparing their class-rooms. Do not overextend meeting times. Keep meetings short; address information that is new, relevant, and of interest to everyone; save the rest for small group meetings. Provide ample time to work in classrooms. Schedule time for beginning teachers and new faculty to meet with their mentors.

Greeting the Students

Some schools have traditional opening exercises or ceremonies. If so, you will probably be expected to deliver a presentation to the students.

Ask your staff about the event, find out what your predecessors did, and determine the role of tradition in this event.

When you prepare your remarks, consider what students want. This is their school, and they want to know how your presence will affect it. Basically, students want to hear (a) admiration for their school, (b) enthusiasm for working with them, (c) any changes in the rules, and (d) reassurance that you will treat them fairly.

When personnel changes occur in schools, students are sometimes provided little or no explanations for those changes. When uninformed, young students sometimes misinterpret the reasons. As several elementary students told one beginning principal, "Our old principal left because he didn't like us." If confusion exists, and you have *permission* to do so, provide a simple, but honest, explanation, such as, "He enjoyed being your principal, but he [retired, moved away, was transferred]."

Meeting the Parents

Most schools have an opening activity that brings parents into the school, such as an open house, curriculum night, or parent–teacher organization meeting. Parents, too, will be anxious to see and hear the new principal. One principal reflected, "I was shocked at the huge crowd at the first parent–teacher meeting. I asked a teacher if the turnout was always so good. 'No,' she answered, 'they're just here to get a look at you.'"

The opening activity provides an opportunity to acknowledge the school's past successes, present a vision for the future, and inspire confidence in you as the school's leader. An effective presentation, according to Ramsey (1999), requires preparation, practice, and forethought. Tips include the following:

- Identify the reason for the presentation—the message.
- Consider needs of the audience: education, culture, background, and interests.
- Believe in your message; use your own words.
- Keep it simple with words that are clear, concise, and precise.
- Use numbered note cards; never read a speech.
- Rehearse; pay attention to timing; speak slowly.
- Videotape your practice sessions; review and revise.
- Check out the location for comfort, seating, and available equipment.
- Use nervous energy to make you animated.
- Plan what to do with your hands; rest them on the podium or gesture appropriately.
- Stand up straight.

- Obtain the audience's attention at the beginning of the presentation.
- Avoid jokes that may offend someone; if in doubt, do not use them.
- Use visual aids when possible.
- Change voice tone, pitch and pace; use pauses for effect.
- Look at members of the audience; make eye contact.
- Provide a memorable ending.

Parents may want to speak to you personally at the end of your presentation. One new principal reported being "bombarded by parents when the program ended. I hadn't anticipated their questions, concerns—even complaints about past issues. As a result, I became flustered." Eliminate the surprise by planning ahead for the possibility. If the conversation moves past socializing, be prepared to respond with, "I'm interested in your [concerns, questions, problems]. However, we need a [quieter, more private] place to talk. Could you call my office tomorrow so we can arrange a time to meet?"

Planning for Public Relations

Whenever you communicate with the public, you influence public perceptions about your school. Thirty years ago a school's public image could rely on publicity—essentially a good newsletter, sports achievements, a few positive stories in the local newspaper, and an active parent organization. Today a more scrutinizing public demands accountability and seeks information from multiple sources. One elementary principal recalls hearing the distinctions described this way:

> When you hang up posters announcing that the circus is coming to town, that's publicity. When you attach a poster to an elephant's rump and parade him through the streets, that's promotion. When you smooth the ruffled feathers of the mayor, whose flowerbed was trampled by the elephant, that's public relations.

Every school has a public image. Ideally, the school's image should be accurate and positive. Some school districts plan for the kind of image they want to project by developing a structured public relations program. These programs provide a means of establishing two-way communication between a school and its constituents. Efforts are made to tell the good news about the school through programs, newsletters, and media reports and to listen to feedback from constituents. If your district has such a program, become familiar with it and participate to the fullest extent.

If your school is not part of a program, consider creating a simple plan for the school. The goal of a public relations plan is two-way communication:

- To share the good news about your school
- To obtain feedback from school constituents.

Of course, a positive image must always be based on a quality educational program.

Share the Good News

The best public relations tools are satisfied consumers. Consequently, parents, students, and personnel are the most credible spokespersons for the school. Other avenues include the following:

- Adopting an eye-catching theme or logo that people will be able to link to your school.

- Maintaining strong internal communications through
    Faculty and staff newsletters
    Faculty and staff meetings
    Accurate and timely information to auxiliary staff, substitute teachers, and student teachers
    Accurate and timely information to students (according to maturity)

- Inviting the external public into the school for
    Open houses
    Student performances
    Student displays
    Science fairs
    Athletic events

- Using a variety of communication tools with external publics
    School newsletters
    News releases
    Newspaper articles
    Radio
    Television
    Public presentations
    Participation in civic organizations
    School Web site
    Flyers
    Brochures
    Personal communication

Ideas to share the good news are limited only by your creativity. Enlist the assistance of faculty and staff. Everyone needs to be actively involved.

Obtain Feedback

Listen to what the school's constituents say about the school. Their perceptions are the reality that they will share with others. If you do not know your constituent's perceptions, you cannot correct incorrect facts or repair misunderstandings. Avenues for obtaining feedback include the following:

- Opening communication lines with the internal public by
  Surveying faculty and staff.
  Debriefing student teachers when they complete their assignments.
  Surveying substitute teachers.
  Talking informally with students.
  Conducting exit interviews with personnel leaving school employment.

- Opening lines of communication with external publics by
  Listening for themes and frequency of compliments, complaints, questions, and rumors.
  Surveying parents.
  Talking with the key communicators in the community.
  Conducting a survey.
  Interviewing community leaders.
  Interviewing local business leaders.

A Checklist for Next Year

Plan for next year by keeping a record of this year. As you formulate plans and prepare for the opening of the school year, maintain a list of plans and copies of all written documents and letters. By doing so, you create a checklist for subsequent planning sessions. Some principals maintain this information in a "summer folder," updating it to provide model documents and an ongoing checklist.

THE END OF THE YEAR

A smooth closure to the school year is equally as important as a smooth beginning. A well-planned closing sends happy students home for the summer and paves the way for a successful opening next year. Plan ahead. The following suggestions provide some ideas for ending the year.

Events

At the end of the year, annual events and ceremonies dominate the calendar. Plays, proms, picnics, parties, and graduations are prominent. Identify each of the events or ceremonies and determine the extent of your responsibility. As one principal pointed out, "There's nothing worse than arriving at an event and finding out that you're expected to give a presentation." Plaques, trophies, and certificates must be prepared in advance of many of these events.

Appreciation

Find out how parent organizations and volunteers are traditionally honored. Carry on whatever tradition exists. If none exists, start one, such as a breakfast, luncheon, or gift plus a personal handwritten thank-you note for the volunteers. Involve teachers and students who benefit from the volunteers' services in planning the occasion.

Think of a way to recognize each teacher and staff member for contributions to the success of the school year. One principal said he "sent each person a handwritten thank you letter, noting the individual's specific contributions." Remember to include members of the maintenance, custodial, cafeteria, and transportation staff. Attend the traditional end of the year gathering for faculty and staff members. If no tradition exists, organize a celebration.

Performance Evaluations

Survey parents to determine their perceptions of the effectiveness of the school and their satisfaction with their children's education. Ask teachers to evaluate your performance.

Principals often fail to conduct these evaluations because they are overwhelmed by the many tasks of the principalship. By simply asking, "How am I doing?" principals can obtain information that will guide their future performance. Two questions posed to parents or to teachers that will yield this information are

- What am I doing that I should continue to do?
- What am I doing that I should no longer do?

Evaluations can be designed based on principal competencies such as

- Interpersonal skills
- Communication
- Decision making
- Planning and organizing

- Supervising and evaluating
- Holding high expectations for students and teachers

Principal evaluations that are based on the principal's goals will provide specific information for the principal. Although designing a specific evaluation requires more effort by the principal, the data from the evaluation will be particularly valuable to the principal.

These evaluations should occur before the frantic activities of closing month. Use the information you gather to improve the school's program as well as your own performance.

Summer Activities

If any groups plan to use the school during the summer or between school terms, find out the details and the persons responsible and make necessary arrangements. Notify maintenance and custodial personnel.

Maintenance and Cleaning

Ask teachers to identify areas in their classrooms that need repair or replacement, such as furniture, blinds, dry-erase boards, lights, and windows. Inventory instructional equipment and identify items that need repair or replacement.

Consult with maintenance and custodial staff to identify building and grounds repairs and improvements that need to be made during the summer. Establish a summer cleaning and repair schedule that takes into account any groups planning to use the building.

Instructional Materials

Collect and account for textbooks and other instructional materials distributed at the beginning of the year. Consult with teachers regarding textbook and instructional needs for the next year.

Planning Ahead

Establish tentative schedules, room assignments, and duty rosters. Share the information with staff members so that they can plan accordingly.

Last Faculty Day

Before teachers leave for the summer, collect grade books, plan books, keys, attendance records, and an inventory of materials left in the classroom.

Be sure teachers have recorded grades and information on students' permanent records. Obtain summer addresses and phone numbers.

THE PRINCIPAL'S KEY

The principal is responsible for setting the tone of the school. A smooth beginning and a carefully planned ending to the school year are reflections of the principal's skills. Through "attention to the details" the principal can design a beginning and an ending that are positive events for all.

4 Learn to Communicate

Communicating, listening, and the ability to build relationships are among the most important skills for a beginning principal.
                              —An elementary principal

Principals spend much of their time interacting with people. The ability to build relationships, generate confidence, and foster trust are essential to establishing leadership. One beginning principal testified, "Developing relationships and earning trust were a challenge . . . I had to work hard to earn both."

At the heart of these human interactions is the art of communication. Strong school leaders are expert communicators. They know that lack of communication and follow-through is a frequent source of faculty and parental discontent. Consequently, they make communication a high priority.

Understanding the varied needs of constituents and determining the form of communication to use are as important as what you say. This chapter examines the issues involved in effective communication.

- The communication system
- The audience
- Needs of the audience
- Communication forms
- Effective strategies

UNDERSTAND THE COMMUNICATION SYSTEM

The principal works with four main constituencies: superintendent and district office staff, school staff, parents, and students. The hierarchical structure of the educational system is reflected in communication patterns. Although communication occurs equally between peers, communication going up the hierarchy is more guarded. Communication going down the hierarchy is likely to be in the form of directives (Sigford, 1998).

KNOW YOUR AUDIENCE

When determining the appropriate form and content of communication for individuals within each group, principals should consider the following questions:

- Who are the members of your audience (maturity, education, experience, language, and culture)?
- What do they need (information, reassurance, support, or motivation)?
- What is their emotional state?
- What is the most appropriate form of communication (personal, group presentation, or written)?

ORGANIZE YOURSELF

The principal's office is a hub of interactions. Visitors, phone calls, e-mails, letters, and memos seem unending. Learning to handle communications expediently and effectively is critical.

A plan to handle routine communications should include the following:

- Secretaries open and sort mail, noting priority items.
- Written communications are prioritized and sorted into folders: today, this week, this month, long range.
- Due dates for reports are noted on the calendar.
- Phones are answered within three rings by courteous, well-trained office personnel who provide accurate information and handle minor issues.
- Phone calls and messages requiring immediate responses are handled as soon as possible.
- Individuals taking messages obtain information about the issue and the individuals involved.
- A time each day is designated for returning phone calls and e-mail messages.
- Phone calls and e-mails are returned within 24 hours.

Parents and teachers are encouraged to make appointments so that there is ample time for their visits.

MAKE PERSONAL COMMUNICATION A PRIORITY

Personal communication is an effective means of building relationships. All members of the school community should feel welcome to talk with the principal. In fact, the principal should seek opportunities to engage individuals in conversation. Two-way communication is the way to solidify relationships, develop trust, and help accomplish goals. One elementary principal emphasized, "Take time to build relationships with staff, teachers, parents, and students. Don't be afraid to admit that you don't know everything and admit it when you make mistakes. You can't command respect, you have to earn it."

COMMUNICATE WITH CONSTITUENTS: THE SUPERINTENDENT AND STAFF

The Superintendent

Regardless of who your supervisor is, establishing a good relationship is critical to retaining your present position and possibly remaining in the profession. The premise for the relationship is that both the principal and the supervisor are capable and qualified to perform their roles. Each is confident of the other's ability. Each knows the other's strengths and weaknesses and showcases those strengths.

Communication between the principal and the superintendent fulfills several functions. First, the superintendent has a broader perspective and greater information than the principal has. The principal, however, has a greater understanding of building-level issues than the superintendent has. The superintendent is responsible to a larger constituency and needs complete information about what is happening in the school district (Schwinden, 1998).

Superintendents value principals whose actions reflect the district's vision and goals and who demonstrate initiative and leadership. They quickly lose confidence in principals who require constant reassurance. Principals must demonstrate the confidence to make independent and daily decisions, keep the superintendent informed on school events, and seek counsel for problems before they are out of control.

Mutual trust is developed through displays of loyalty and support. Each party can depend on the other. As one principal explained, "I completely trusted my boss. When he hired me, we made a pact that we would support each other 100 percent. We agreed to communicate regularly, disagree in private, and publicly support each other's decisions."

Although allegiance to an employer is central to effective leadership, allegiance to personal values is central to personal wellness. If your values conflict with the values espoused by the school district or the superintendent, it is time to seek a different position.

District Staff

When you receive district directives, convey the information with respect and accuracy. Address any differences of opinion with superiors in private. Date and prioritize requests for information from the central office. Although secretarial or other administrative staff may assist in assembling information, the responsibility for the content and its timeliness belongs to the principal. Remember, the superintendent's secretary is the gatekeeper to the superintendent.

COMMUNICATE WITH SCHOOL PERSONNEL

As the school's principal, your communications with teachers and staff members takes on new meaning. You will be regarded as an authority figure. Teachers may be guarded and less than forthright in their communications with you. For a beginning principal, unaccustomed to being viewed as an authority figure, this may be a surprise and a disappointment. According to one beginning principal, "I had to assess my communication strategies . . . to become less straightforward and intimidating."

Building Understanding

Some principals use personality assessment tools, such as the Myers-Briggs typology, to assist them in opening dialogues and improving relationships among their staff. Most personality assessments are designed to measure personal attributes, such as behavior, attitudes, opinions, motivation, interests, and values. To be effective, staff members should participate voluntarily, understand the purpose of the assessment, and know how results will be reported and used.

Benefits of personality assessment include the following:

- Principals and staff members gain understanding of personal strengths and weaknesses.
- Staff members gain appreciation of their colleagues' strengths and talents.
- Principals learn the kinds of performance feedback that staff members will accept.

Personality assessment can facilitate

- Improved communication
- Better relationships
- Reduced conflict
- Improved performance

Properly selected and administered, an assessment tool may provide useful information. Don't forget, however, that an assessment tool presents a single piece of information about an individual on a given day. There is no substitute for the information gathered by a principal through daily interactions with staff members.

A word of caution: A beginning principal should obtain authorization and guidance from district officials before selecting or using any assessment instrument with staff members.

Keeping Teachers Informed

The principal's job is to enforce policies and procedures so teachers can teach. Although teachers want to be informed, they do not want to be bombarded with administrative trivia and directives that do not involve them. If information will have a personal or professional impact on teachers or support staff, tell them the parts that they need to know. Decide which ommunication method is best suited for the situation.

Memos

When information is self-explanatory, send a memo. Make the memo brief, clearly written, and to the point. When a response if required, include a deadline. Be sure the tone of the memo is positive and cordial.

Meetings

If the information disseminated will be questioned or require discussion and decision making, hold a meeting. Meetings should be held only when

- A specific purpose exists.
- A specific conclusion is the goal of the meeting.
- No other form of communication is adequate.
- Input from others is necessary or desired.

Effective meetings are based on the following:

- Advance notice is provided to the participants.
- Meeting times are convenient for the participants.
- The purpose of the meeting is stated.

- Agendas (including items suggested by participants) are distributed in advance.
- Agendas include starting and ending times.
- A designated person records the minutes of the meeting.
- Meetings adhere to agenda items and times. The principal is responsible for starting on time, keeping the meeting focused, the discussion pace, and ending the meeting on time.
- All participants freely exchange ideas. Each person's ideas are sought.
- A specific conclusion is reached.
- The principal provides a summary statement.
- Follow-up steps are identified.

Minutes of the meeting are verified for accuracy and distributed to all participants.

Committees

"Let's turn it over to a committee," often resounds at the conclusion of a meeting. Consequently, committees often become the "dumping grounds" for problems and dilemmas that elude obvious solutions. Committees that are mishandled waste time and energy, postpone solutions, and create larger problems. Committees that are handled effectively, however, can be constructive.

The principal must (a) limit the number of committees, (b) establish committees that have a purpose and the potential to fulfill their mission, (c) provide adequate resources, (d) avoid interference, and (e) use the information, decisions, or recommendations of the committee.

The elements of an effective committee include the following:

- A leader
- A specific task
- An expected outcome
- A target date for task completion
- Small, carefully selected membership with term limits
- Adequate resources
- Authority
- Records of proceedings
- Scheduled progress reports

The Daily Bulletin

Schools operate more smoothly when everyone is aware of school events and activities. An event that appears to involve only one class or a small group may affect many others. A daily bulletin, distributed electronically or in mailboxes, or displayed in a central place is a way to keep everyone informed. Remember to include part-time teachers, auxiliary staff, volunteers, student teachers, cafeteria workers, bus drivers, and grounds and custodial staff in the distribution of the information.

Some principals include staff birthdays, family events, personal accomplishments, and humorous happenings in the bulletin. Note the following cautions if you report personal information about staff members: (a) the potential for missing someone or something, (b) offending someone with unwanted attention, and (c) the possibility of students, parents, and visitors reading the information. A safer route is sticking to school news.

When Staff Share Personal Problems

School leadership sometimes involves listening to the personal problems of staff members. The principal may be viewed as a sympathetic listener or a trusted source of guidance. Sometimes staff members need to discuss personal circumstances that affect their work. In any case, some beginning principals are surprised and feel ill prepared for this role.

When minor or temporary problems are presented, the appropriate response is to listen and facilitate the staff member's problem solving. Unresolved personal problems can affect work performance. Serious personal problems, beyond the scope of a principal's training, should be directed to appropriate professionals. Occasionally, staff members will resist the suggestion of professional help, but concern for the welfare of the staff member and the school should guide the principal's responses.

Principals should not take ownership of staff members' personal problems. One principal cautioned, "I wanted everyone to like me, so I encouraged them to share their problems. I took on the problems of everyone. Soon I had teachers calling me at 10 o'clock at night. I was in over my head."

Occasionally staff problems border on the ludicrous. One principal recalled,

The day was a 10 on the crazy scale. People were lined up outside the office and the phone was ringing off the wall. I was short a teacher, as the first-grade teacher had gone home, announcing that her "thoughtless rat of a husband" was out of town fishing and her baby was sick. In the midst of the chaos, the kindergarten teacher arrived announcing she had a problem to discuss with me. In a most serious tone, she began, "I am having problems with odor in my cat's litter box. Could you suggest a good litter?"

COMMUNICATE WITH STUDENTS

Although students are the reason schools exist, they are often neglected in the communication process. Communicating with students, formally and informally, will provide access to their perspective on the school and on student life. The most effective communication may occur during impromptu meetings in the hallway or cafeteria. Some principals schedule regular visits with students. Examples include eating with them in the cafeteria, walking around on the playground, inviting those with birthdays to the office, or becoming a temporary student in a science or art class. Other opportunities include greeting students in the morning and as they leave at the end of the day.

Student requests to meet with the principal merit the same courtesy and consideration given to adults. Students should feel comfortable during appointments with the principal or when dropping by to say hello.

Often principals are the only people students trust when serious problems occur. As one elementary principal recalled,

> One day a little girl came to my office complaining that her ear hurt. She wanted me to "fix it." Under her long hair, I discovered bruises on the back of her ear and neck. She explained, "I wasn't the only one who was naughty . . . mommy was hitting everyone."

Now and then enterprising students request meetings to discuss school improvement. When feasible, their projects should be undertaken. One principal said,

> I was surprised at how innovative young children could be. One year the third graders had aspirations for great changes. One group wanted to recycle milk cartons; another group wanted to lobby the school board for new playground equipment. They came prepared with proposals, rationales, and procedures for launching their projects.

Disciplinary meetings with students can be challenging. Strong emotions can impede problem solving. Students need to be given time to calm themselves before discussion can occur. Principals may need to postpone meetings until the inappropriate behavior can be addressed calmly.

COMMUNICATE WITH PARENTS

The term "parents" is used in this book to identify the head of a family. Principals need to remember that not all students live with a mother and father. Someone other than a biological parent may fill the parent role. Family may include many special relationships. The wording of communications should be broad enough to embrace the diversity of student's homes.

Parents and guardians become acquainted with a principal through the communications sent from the school, the principal's presentations at meetings, and personal conversations. In a large school, it is difficult to meet every parent. However, the principal should try to meet and establish relationships with as many school families as possible.

Building a trusting relationship with parents requires effective communication between the principal, teacher, and parents. What kinds of communication do parents want?

1. They want communication that is frequent, reliable, and two-way.

2. They want opportunities to share information and opinions.

3. They want to hear about their child's progress and not always just the negative side. Include good news about their child as well.

4. They want information about the school policies, programs, and schedules.

5. They want information about classroom activities.

Although most parents welcome the opportunity to get acquainted with the principal, some parents may have had prior, unhappy school experiences. They may be intimidated or hostile toward the principal. One elementary principal observed, "As a new principal I was amazed when some parents seemed reluctant to meet with me. I had a hard time imagining myself as intimidating." Another beginning principal commented, "Some parents seemed angry and defiant the first time I met them." She added jokingly, "They could at least wait until I did something wrong before they attacked me." Acknowledge past problems if parents mention them and try to make their experiences with you favorable. They may become your most loyal supporters, as this principal experienced:

> I sought opportunities to speak personally with parents who appeared to harbor some hostility toward the school. I invited them to participate on committees and volunteer in classrooms. Over time, they began to trust me. Eventually some of them became my most loyal supporters.

Establishing a communication schedule, such as monthly bulletins, weekly classroom updates, quarterly conferences, and daily homework folders, assists parents in anticipating information and planning for school events. Take every opportunity to greet and talk with parents when they visit the school. Invite parents to visit the school for student performances and open houses.

Consider educational levels and language differences when sending information to student's homes. Sending information home with students does not ensure its arrival. Important or confidential information should be mailed. One principal recalled sending mail special delivery to the parents of one "mailbox raider."

Points to consider when sending written communications to parents:

- Have a reason to write.
- Communicate in writing only if it is the most effective way to communicate the message.
- Identify the message that you want to convey.
- Consider the needs of the audience.
- Use clear, concise, and precise words.
- Avoid technical terms, slang, and acronyms.
- Stick to the point.
- Be brief.
- Edit, edit, edit. Have someone else proofread.
- Create your own templates for frequently used letters, memos, bulletins, and newsletters.
- Ask for assistance from a public relations specialist if necessary.

Family Secrets

Sometimes family members reveal serious problems during conferences with the principal. Beginning principals are often surprised and disarmed when marital, financial, medical, and even criminal issues are divulged.

Family members may share sensitive information simply to make the principal aware of the student's home situation. This information is confidential unless a student is in danger or needs specific assistance. The principal may need to suggest professional help. Discuss confidentiality issues with parents, so that they do not feel their trust has been violated if you seek assistance for the student.

Sometimes parents request information that a principal is not at liberty to share. Student and faculty confidentiality rights may conflict with a parent's desire for information. Be truthful in what you say, but reveal only what is appropriate.

THE PRINCIPAL'S KEY

For the beginning principal, the time and care invested in developing communication processes and opportunities is well spent. Schooling is a "people business" and is based on human interactions. The skilled principal masters and fosters the art of communication.

5 Maximize Staff Potential

The task of the leader is to get his people from where they are to where they have not been.

—Henry Kissinger

The key to an excellent school is an outstanding staff. The principal's role is to create that outstanding staff by maximizing the potential of each staff member.

Most teachers are dedicated people who are motivated to work harder and longer than their job contract or job description requires. They have a sense of duty and loyalty to a cause that extends beyond their classrooms or work assignments, to the entire school and the education profession. Some teachers tend to overwork and may need assistance in avoiding job overload. For the principal, the task of facilitating their continued growth is enjoyable.

A small percentage of staff members, however, may not be dedicated to the profession. Instead, they are mediocre, marginal, or difficult employees. They are recognizable by the numbers of (a) requests for student transfers from their classes, (b) student discipline referrals they generate, and (c) parent and student complaints about them. The more vocal of these teachers will resist change, undermine school efforts, negatively influence other staff members, and fill the faculty lounge with gossip and complaints. If they are informal leaders of the faculty, the problem is especially difficult.

Improving the teaching performance and attitudes of mediocre and negative teachers is the principal's responsibility. No student deserves a mediocre or an uncaring teacher. Negative teachers tarnish the perceptions of the school and principal.

To create an outstanding staff:

1. Be a role model of motivation and enthusiasm.

2. Set high expectations.

3. Provide personal attention.

4. Identify individual talents and potential.

5. Assign responsibilities according to training and education so that success is possible.

6. Recognize and praise accomplishments.

7. Delegate; share decisions that affect staff members.

8. Encourage and facilitate professional development.

Apply the classical theories of McGregor, Herzberg, and Maslow to the approaches and strategies used with the staff.

1. Assume that all people are basically ambitious, trustworthy, and want to succeed. Hire the best people and communicate high expectations (McGregor, 1960).

2. Understand that people will be minimally satisfied by pay, working conditions, and fringe benefits but that they are motivated when they like their job, receive recognition, and have opportunities for growth and advancement (Herzberg, 1987).

3. Remember that in addition to job security, a paycheck, and a safe work environment, employees want to belong socially, to feel that they and their work are valued, and to achieve self-fulfillment from their work (Maslow, 1954).

COMMUNICATE EXPECTATIONS

Clearly State Expectations

One beginning principal reported, "Unfortunately, I made the mistake of using the word 'might' when stating my expectations. My 'expectations' were interpreted as mere suggestions."

Model Expectations

Actions speak loudly. Staff members watch and measure the principal's level of enthusiasm, work ethic, and dedication as well as what the principal notices and rewards.

A motivated staff begins with a motivated leader. Bulach, Pickett, and Boothe (1998) suggested avoiding the following behaviors:

- Displaying an uncaring attitude
- Being distant, not circulating, or not calling staff members by name
- Failing to encourage and compliment
- Failing to trust
- Refusing to delegate

Provide Personal Attention

> *Make an investment in people . . . of time, your interest, and your advocacy.*
> —An elementary principal

A critical factor in employee motivation and satisfaction is personal attention from the principal (Brock & Grady, 2000, 2001). Consequently, the principal must provide personal attention to each person in the work setting.

Take the time to develop a relationship with each staff member. Make a point of talking with each person every day. Establish an ongoing dialogue. Develop extensive personal information about the staff. Learn each person's strengths, weaknesses, talents, abilities, needs, and aspirations. Use that information to motivate and guide individual development.

Be aware of your interpersonal skills. Sometimes principals do not recognize their deficiencies in interpersonal relationships, particularly those principals who have strong task orientations. As one principal said, "I was certain that I was people oriented and had excellent human relation skills until I surveyed my staff at the end of my first year. I was shocked when the entire staff reported that I was too focused on tasks and ignored the needs of the people."

Identify Individual Needs, Talents, and Potential

Discover the strategies that will bring forth the best in each staff member. Which staff members need personal attention? Which teachers need coaching? Who will thrive on new challenges? Who will blossom with more leadership? Who is trustworthy? Who requires careful monitoring? Who needs remediation? Who needs to be counseled into another career? (Torre, 1999).

Assign Responsibilities for Which Employees Have Been Trained

Staff members need to be assigned according to their training. Individuals who are assigned to areas outside their training are "set up" for frustration and failure.

Recognize and Praise Accomplishments

Notice efforts and praise accomplishments. Teachers receive little adult recognition for their daily efforts in classrooms. Custodians clean up one mess only to move on to another. Words of appreciation, praise, and recognition are the "currency" of a positive work environment.

Delegate

> *Establish yourself as a teachable person—one who believes she can learn from everyone.*
>
> —An elementary principal

The principal must master the ability to delegate. Successful leaders identify and develop the talents and potential of followers. One means of doing that is by delegating leadership opportunities to others. Obviously, you will need to match the task and abilities of the employee, describe the assignment carefully, and be available for consultation.

Although delegation includes some risk, the benefits far surpass the disappointments. Delegation communicates to employees that they are trusted and valued. Used properly, delegation is a powerful motivational tool.

Share Decision Making

> *An "attitude of my school, my teachers, my ideas" should be avoided.*
> —A beginning principal

No principal can be expert at teaching all grades and subjects, running an office, and maintaining a building. It makes sense to involve staff members in making decisions about issues in their areas of expertise. Invite staff members to participate in making decisions that will affect them. People are more satisfied and work harder when they have a voice in decisions. At the same time, do not burden teachers with decisions that rightfully belong to you. Individuals who are involved in making decisions will be prepared to implement the decisions.

ENCOURAGE AND FACILITATE PROFESSIONAL DEVELOPMENT

The quality and quantity of student learning is directly proportionate to the dedication and skill of the teachers. To maintain a professional edge, teachers require a sustained program of renewal and reflection. They need to work in a community where lifelong learning is a priority and underlying theme.

When teachers fail to grow professionally, they lose their motivation. Their teaching suffers; their students fail to learn. With the luster of teaching gone, some teachers leave the profession. Others remain on the job, burned out and unproductive.

Principals have long been aware of the need for professional development, but the traditional professional development model of workshops and conferences needs to be replaced. After years of exposure to one-day workshops that had little relevance to their work, teachers are skeptical when new ideas and programs are presented.

Teachers do not emerge from college with all the teaching skills they need for the duration of their careers. The art of teaching is a developmental progress that begins during preservice education and continues throughout a career. A professional development program should be tailored to meet the needs of the developing teacher in the context of the school culture. When teachers chart their own course, the results are more likely to have a positive and long-term impact on their teaching.

In this model, the principal acts as facilitator and teachers take responsibility for their own development. In consultation with the principal, the teachers select professional growth goals that are consistent with the standards for their teaching field and design a course of action to meet those goals. The principal facilitates the teacher's endeavor by providing ongoing

- Consultation
- Encouragement
- Resources
- Time to reflect, plan, and observe others
- Opportunities for collaboration with peers
- Periodic progress reviews
- Evaluation

This process requires a commitment of time from the principal. Given the impact of teachers on student learning, however, professional development of teachers should be a high priority. Additional information on professional development can be found in *From First-Year to First-Rate: Principals Guiding Beginning Teachers* (Brock & Grady, 2001).

SUSTAIN STAFF MORALE

Although motivation involves employees' desire to achieve their best, morale refers to their overall workplace experience. Motivation will not be sustained if the workplace is not satisfying. Employees can have high morale, like where they work, but not have high motivation. One principal said, "I was delighted to join a school where the faculty was one big happy family. However, I soon discovered that while they were very congenial, they were not highly motivated toward collegial professional growth."

Here is one teacher's advice to sustain workplace morale:

Smile, call us by name. Act like you care and know what's important to us. Bring small groups of teachers together to work on tasks. Provide positive feedback. Use conflict resolution to resolve issues. Survey the faculty regularly to find out what people have to say and how things are improving. Be in the classrooms and point out good things that are happening—specific things. Don't patronize. Be available. If you see someone in distress, unhappy, and retreating from others, reach out and help them. (Brock & Grady, 2000, p. 57)

The following workplace strategies are recommended:

1. Provide uninterrupted time to teach.

2. Minimize duties. Examine current school practices and eliminate nonessential paperwork and duties.

3. Maximize encouragement. Teachers have no measure of quality at the end of the day other than a student's response and an occasional compliment from a parent. Teachers rely on reinforcement from principals (Blase & Kirby, 1992; Brock & Grady, 2000). Offer frequent, but sincere and specific, praise for accomplishments and effort. Encourage and reward new ideas. Spend time talking with teachers; listen to their concerns and issues. Leave notes of encouragement in their mailboxes.

4. Show concern for individuals. Smile, get to know staff, greet them by name.

5. Provide recognition. Notice and acknowledge accomplishments and efforts.

6. Treat people fairly. Do not show favoritism.

7. Be enthusiastic. The principal is the school's cheerleader.

8. Communicate. Tell teachers what is happening. Give them opportunities to provide input.

9. Share. Engage teachers in decisions that affect them.

10. Grant autonomy in how work is accomplished.

11. Be supportive. Teachers need unwavering support when they experience problems with parents or community. Sometimes this support will take the form of *privately* helping a teacher recognize and correct a mistake.

12. Encourage professional growth through supervision and staff development.

13. Maintain a clean and orderly school environment.

14. Be decisive. Reach a decision and follow through. (Brock & Grady, 2000)

Share Your Expectations

The teachers do not "know you" as the principal. They cannot know your expectations unless you explain them. The first three to six months is the opportune time for beginning principals to communicate their expectations (Hart, 1993). The principal must describe the vision for a successful school, quality teaching, and a good education.

Staff members must be told that excellence is expected. The definition of excellence and examples of excellence must be communicated to the teachers. Share your confidence in their ability to achieve excellence. You will find that people perform at the level expected of them.

Be Equitable

Be equitable in the treatment of staff members. Favoritism is quickly recognized and resented. Relationships, cooperation, and staff commitment are eroded in an environment where favoritism prevails; resentment, competition, and jealousy emerge.

Each staff member may have different needs, but the principal must apply the same rules and maintain an equitable division of work and provide opportunities for all staff members.

Be Consistent

The principal's behavior and words must match. Actions speak louder than words. When contradictory, actions are believed. For instance, if the principal announces that innovative teaching is valued, yet teachers who try new ideas are not supported, then the principal's words will not be believed. Support words with actions or behaviors.

Be Flexible and Understanding

Adopt an attitude of service.
> —An elementary principal's advice

The principal enforces employment contract requirements and district work regulations. Staff members are responsible adults, however, and unless otherwise indicated, they should be treated as professionals. Most adults will meet or exceed work expectations. Life sometimes interferes with rules. When it does, be flexible. Show understanding. One principal gave this example:

> A teacher who had always been on time, suddenly started arriving a few minutes late. I called her to my office intending to reprimand her. Luckily, I began the conversation with, "I notice that lately you're having a problem arriving on time. That's not like you. Is there something wrong at home?" She tearfully told me that her spouse had become seriously ill. Her family was in crisis. Schedules were disrupted. She needed help, not a reprimand.

Keep Your Cool

Nothing destroys the climate of a school faster than a principal who displays emotional mood swings. Teachers and students do not know what to expect. Office staff feel compelled to "test the waters" before approaching the principal.

Learn to maintain a consistent emotional level. Although you are bound to feel upset, angry, or even depressed, learn to detach yourself emotionally and control your behavior. Your staff members have enough problems of their own without being subject to your bad moods. Deal with your emotions when other people are not present. Never lose your temper, chastise a staff member publicly, or speak unkindly about students or parents.

One principal recalled, "I had given little thought to my effect on people until one day I overheard a teacher remark that whenever we talked, it lifted her spirits. After that, I made a conscious effort to speak with each person every day."

Be Visible

Teachers want a principal who knows what is going on—who spends time where the action is. If you spend all your time in the office, you will not know what is happening in the school. The staff will assume that you are not interested in what they are doing.

Instead, drop in on classes. Do not interrupt, just pop in and out. Students and teachers will become accustomed to your presence. One elementary principal said, "I told each class at the beginning of the year that I would be stopping by. Knowing how easily young children are distracted, I told the children and teacher that they should continue with whatever they were doing." After a brief visit, make a point of visiting with the teacher or drop a note in the teacher's mailbox commenting on some positive learning activities that you observed. Any constructive criticism should be accompanied by positive observations delivered in a personal conversation.

Praise Accomplishments

If I was beginning my career again, the one thing I would do more of is praise teachers more for their efforts and accomplishments.
—An elementary principal

Telling teachers what they do well bolsters their confidence, acknowledges their worth, and lets them know what you value. Personal praise has the most value. Watch for behaviors and practices that should be replicated and praise staff members for them. Be honest and specific in the praise. "Good job" and "nice work" do not tell people what behavior to repeat. Saying, "You certainly captured the interest of your students with your science demonstration today," commends the teacher on a precise practice. Telling the custodian "I appreciate how clean you keep the windows in the school" indicates what practice should be continued.

Praising individuals in front of a group is risky. The recipient of the praise may be uncomfortable being singled out, and those in the audience may become resentful. When individual accomplishments are noted in front of a group or in a school newsletter, make a practice of mentioning everyone of the staff members at some time. Avoid praising the same people repeatedly.

Let Each Person Know

Establish a spirit of teamwork, one in which every person who works in the school feels that he or she is vital to the school's success. When individuals believe that they are contributors to a collective goal, their work becomes more meaningful, and the quality improves. Acknowledge each person's role and worth. Teachers, office staff, custodians, cafeteria workers, bus drivers, and auxiliary staff need to know the importance of their roles in the education of students. One principal provided this example:

When I thanked my new custodian for working above and beyond the call of duty, he explained that he worked hard because he felt like he was part of a team—that he played a role in the education of the students. He became the best custodian I ever had.

Place Teachers Where They Shine

Teachers will do their best work when they are placed in the right grade level and teach the right subject. Sometimes potentially good teachers do not do as well as they could or should because they have the wrong placement— even the wrong school. Some teachers stagnate by remaining at the same grade level or teaching the same classes too long.

Suggest a grade level or assignment change for teachers whose creativity is lagging or whose productivity does not match their potential. Without a change, they may not recognize their untapped abilities. Sometimes teachers begin their careers teaching a certain grade and then stay at the same grade throughout their careers without ever considering that they might be better suited for another grade. One principal reported, "When teachers request changes in grade levels or in the classes they teach, I try to make it happen. Sometimes I recommend, even encourage it. They are usually surprised and pleased with their renewed enthusiasm and success."

Forgive and Forget

Meet people with an open mind. Do not make decisions about a staff member based on rumors or previous evaluations. Obviously, if a termination or remediation process is already underway, you will need to follow district procedures. Otherwise, give everyone an opportunity to begin with a clean slate. People can and will change.

Insist on Respect

Show respect to all members of the school community and insist that your staff members do the same. Your behavior will provide a model. No purpose is served when conflict becomes personal. Instead, agree to disagree about issues without becoming disrespectful.

Be Supportive

Teachers expect principals to support their actions and decisions when a conflict develops. In most cases, supporting a teacher's decisions is not a problem. Principals should intercede with angry parents and support teachers.

When a teacher has made a serious error in judgment, however, principals face a dilemma. Care must be taken to ensure that the teacher's actions cause no harm to the student. At the same time, the principal must enable the teacher to save face while negotiating with angry parents. If the teacher perceives that the principal is siding with a complaining parent or student, trust between the principal and the teacher disappears. Consequently, it is important to inform teachers of your position on support before a problem develops.

Trust

Trust is earned through mutual honesty, communication, and respect. When trust exists between the principal and the faculty, teachers are more likely to trust one another, collaborate, and be committed to school goals.

SUPERVISION AND EVALUATION

People need and deserve feedback about the quality of their performance. The principal's ability to provide feedback enhances the quality of education provided in the school.

Become familiar with the supervision and evaluation process used in the school district. For daily supervision and summative evaluations, the following documents may serve as guides:

1. The job description (each employee in the school community should have a job description)

2. Contract stipulations

3. The goals of the district and the school

4. A set of individual goals determined cooperatively by the staff member and principal

Supervision by Wandering

Although most schools have a process for scheduled classroom observations, a principal learns much by wandering the halls and dropping by classrooms. A "staged" performance is not as accurate as what happens daily inside the classroom. When visiting classrooms, be careful not to interrupt the teacher or distract the students.

One principal said,

I tried to stop by each teacher's classroom every day, even if it was only for a few moments. I left brief notes about positive observations in mailboxes. If I saw something that wasn't acceptable, I made a point of speaking to the person. When I returned to my office, I made brief notes, documenting incidents and examples that I could use for end of the year performance evaluations and goal setting.

Ignoring Behavior Condones It

Not every teacher makes good decisions.
—A beginning high school principal

If unacceptable behavior is observed during "wandering," the principal has a responsibility to respond to the behavior. If the teacher knows that the principal is aware of the unacceptable behavior, ignoring it condones the behavior (Whitaker, 1999). Address the behavior quietly, so others cannot hear, in a nonconfrontational manner, such as, "I noticed you left your class unattended, is something wrong?" Without being accusatory, let the teacher know that the behavior is not appropriate.

Dealing With Difficult Teachers

One of my most difficult challenges was dealing with mediocre teachers. When you're on the other side of the desk it's easy to say, 'Why don't they get rid of him or her?' But when you're the administrator, you realize it's not that simple. You have to look at the big picture. Then you realize that he or she is not bad enough to get rid of, but not good either . . . just mediocre.
—A middle school principal

The teachers who present the most challenges are those who are mediocre, marginal, or negative. They have probably been allowed to persist in these behaviors for a long time. Changing the behavior will be difficult.

To change a behavior, first determine why it exists. Most people want to (a) feel successful, (b) be part of a group, (c) have their work valued, (d) feel that their work is important, and (e) be recognized for their efforts. People behave badly when their needs are not being met. Develop a relationship, establish a dialogue, and discover how the teacher feels. Determine if the teacher

1. Lacks the skills to teach. If so, retrain or coach.

2. Is in the wrong placement. If so, change grade levels, subject areas, or schools.

3. Feels left out of the group. Is the person part of a minority group (gender, color, ethnicity)? Encourage informal socialization.

4. Feels that the school or community does not value the subjects that he or she teaches (e.g., Latin in a community that values sports and vocational education).

5. Is suffering burnout. Mediocre teachers who were previously high performers may be struggling with burnout. Additional information on burnout is available in *Rekindling the Flame: Principals Combating Teacher Burnout* (Brock & Grady, 2000).

6. Has untapped talents or needs new challenges.

7. Previously worked in a negative climate. Establish the climate of a winning team.

8. Feels unrecognized for hard work and successes. Provide recognition.

9. Needs to be counseled into more appropriate employment (Brock & Grady, 2000).

Once the behavior's cause is determined, jolt the teacher out of the comfort zone. Assume the teacher wants to do well, let the teacher know the expectations. Provide whatever remediation is needed: retraining, changed assignments, new challenges, opportunities to participate or team up with a high achiever. The solution will be unique for each individual.

Teachers who are negative or create conflicts with students and parents, require quick interventions. The negative perception that they can create for the school and their effect on colleagues is damaging. Additionally, they are quick to assume informal leadership positions on the faculty, further damaging staff morale.

Do not give negative teachers power by allowing them to interfere with plans or progress. Proceed with plans and activities in spite of their negativity. Assign these teachers a responsibility and assume that they will follow through. Do not reinforce their behavior by allowing them to shirk their duty. If the negative teacher is an informal leader, assign a leadership role to the teacher and expect results (Whitaker, 1999).

Misery loves company. Negative teachers tend to cluster together to complain, moan, and criticize. Make it difficult for them to gather and solicit new members. Team negative teachers with highly dedicated teachers for responsibilities, planning periods, playground duty, and cafeteria times.

Beginning Teachers

Protect beginning teachers from teachers who are negative or ineffective. Inadequate teacher induction is a precipitating factor in the development of mediocrity and negativity. Without assistance, the goal of beginning teachers is survival. They adopt the first teaching skills that work. Without additional assistance, they develop no further than their early survival skills. The frustrations and disappointments of the early years create disillusionment and negativity.

To help beginning teachers become superior teachers, (a) provide appropriate induction during the first years of their teaching and (b) continue with planned, sequential, professional development. For additional information, consult *From First-Year to First-Rate: Principals Guiding Beginning Teachers* (Brock & Grady, 2001).

Records

In your record of observations, be certain that the information is based on observable behaviors and not subjective judgments. All feedback provided to personnel should be based on observable—preferably quantifiable—behaviors and shared with the individuals concerned. Document, date, and file the results of all supervisory conferences. Share the information that is destined for personnel files with the individuals concerned. If personnel information is saved on your computer's hard drive, be certain to have a secure password and that nobody else has access to that computer.

Performance Goals

Teachers may reuse the same goals year after year. Their goals may be hastily written to fulfill the district's goal-setting requirement and then forgotten.

Work with teachers to develop goals that will improve their performance. Prepare goals written in measurable terms. Identify benchmarks that will signify that a goal has been met. Throughout the year, schedule time with teachers to review the goals and check on progress. During appraisals, ask teachers for indicators of goal accomplishment.

Self-Evaluation

Encourage staff members to engage in self-evaluation. Although self-evaluation does not substitute for formal evaluation, it does require that teachers critically review their own behaviors and progress. Ask teachers to identify areas of strength and areas of needed improvement. People are more willing to improve when they identify and acknowledge the need. The information teachers provide suggests how they perceive themselves and their work.

Evaluation Traps

Many principals dread completing teacher evaluations. Summarizing a person's work contributions is exceptionally complex. Principals may fall into the following common traps:

- *Leniency.* Giving everybody a good evaluation so that no one's feelings are hurt or to avoid making waves.
- *Downgrading.* Always finding something wrong because if people have high evaluations, they have nothing to improve.
- *Subjectivity.* Giving people they like better evaluations than those they do not like.
- *Laziness.* Writing the same thing as on the previous year's evaluation.
- *Narrow-mindedness.* Concentrating the evaluation on one positive or negative incident or basing the evaluation on an incident that occurred during the last few months rather than the entire academic year.

Evaluations such as these do not measure and reflect a person's work performance. They are worthless and insulting to the teachers. Instead:

- Gather information all year.
- Consider each person's work record for the entire academic year.
- Be objective.
- Provide ratings supported by verifiable data.
- Use the information to facilitate the individual's growth.

Inappropriate Behavior

Most beginning principals dread reprimanding a teacher for inappropriate behavior. Inevitably, however, somebody will speak rudely to a parent, punish a student inappropriately, leave school early, or arrive late.

Regardless of the incident, it is important to act promptly. Ignoring a situation signals either acceptance of the inappropriate behavior or weakness.

First, gather irrefutable evidence that inappropriate behavior occurred. Speak with the person privately and calmly. If the incident is serious, inform the superintendent before doing so. Focus on the behavior that was observed and the policy that prohibits it. Be constructive. The goal is to correct future behavior, not punish the offender. As one beginning principal advised, "Let people retain their dignity."

1. Inform the individual of the behavior that was objectionable.

2. Note the supporting district policy.

3. Explain the behavior change that is required.

4. Outline the steps required.

5. Give the person an opportunity to state his or her position.

6. Reiterate the policy that supports the behavior change.

7. Offer assistance if appropriate.

8. Provide an appropriate timeframe for the change to occur.

9. Provide documentation in accordance with district policies and procedures.

Some teachers should not be teaching. For these individuals, today's disciplinary problems may become grounds for termination; termination can become grounds for legal action. It is essential to follow school district policies and procedures in the following situations:

1. Conduct that requires immediate dismissal

2. Conduct that requires notification of law enforcement authorities

3. Conduct that requires a disciplinary conference

4. Repeated inappropriate conduct

Leave a "paper trail" to document that the situation was handled according to district policies and procedures. Keep files on all cases. Do not discuss any information about a disciplined employee with anyone other than school or legal authorities.

THE PRINCIPAL'S KEY

Building the best staff possible is the principal's challenge. It is through staff members that excellence is achieved in the school.

The principal must encourage the professional development of teachers and focus on their strengths. By being a positive role model and developing a culture of high expectations, a teaching environment of success and possibility is created.

When staff problems exist, they cannot be ignored. The principal must intervene to assist staff members who are experiencing difficulties.

6 Use Time Effectively

It wasn't as easy as I thought it would be to find time to do the things that a good principal does, such as interact with teachers, visit with students, and observe classrooms—all those things you have to get out of your office to do. It's hard to get out of your office!

—A middle school principal

Time is a major problem for all principals, but especially for beginners. Everything is new, and doing things for the first time takes longer. During the second year, a principal will feel more comfortable, but time management continues to be a challenge.

Principals have staggering workloads. Since it is unlikely that work demands will decrease, learning efficient work strategies is the best solution.

Everyone has the same amount of time. Some principals, however, know how to get more done in a day. They know how to manage their time efficiently and effectively. A beginner has the advantage of developing time-saving strategies without having to overcome old, bad habits.

ORGANIZE THE OFFICE

The environment can decrease efficiency if it is uncomfortable or inconvenient. Equip the office with a suitable desk, comfortable desk chair, ample storage, appropriate technology, and adequate lighting. Arrange the furniture so that items that are used daily are conveniently located. Position the workspace so that it is not visible to people entering the outer office. This will reduce distractions as well as discourage passersby from dropping in to chat.

Keep the Desk and Office Tidy

Keep the desktop uncluttered. Assign a place for everything, and make it a practice to put things where they belong. Principals who work in rubble, lose things, waste precious time hunting for them, and convey a message of dubious leadership ability.

Wisely Discard

Examine the information left in the office by predecessors. Place unneeded or unwanted items in a storage closet. Do not be hasty in discarding documents and records. Information that seems unimportant today may take on new importance at a later time. Ask the secretary about questionable files.

Arrange for Visitors

Arrange a place to meet with visitors. Having a conference table is ideal. If the office is small, two chairs and a small table or a chair next to the desk may be sufficient. Avoid the authoritarian image of sitting behind a desk for meetings. Try to arrange chairs for visitors away from the doorway to provide privacy.

Use the Computer Wisely

The computer can save time if used properly. The time spent becoming computer literate reaps valuable rewards. Purchase and install identical software so that home and work computers can interface. Duplicate files from the hard drive onto disks so that projects can be completed at home.

Used appropriately, computers are timesavers and allies; used inappropriately, they become time wasters and enemies. Some words of caution:

1. Keep electronic data stored on the hard drive secure by using a password, and store floppy disks and CDs in a locked storage cabinet.

2. Remember that surfing the Internet is not a private activity.

3. Remember that e-mail is not private. It can be saved, printed, or forwarded to any number of people with a single command. Deleting e-mail does not erase it. Beware of e-mail messages becoming headlines.

4. Rules of grammar, spelling, and courtesy have as much application to electronic mail as to other forms of written correspondence.

5. Keep professional and personal e-mail on separate accounts.

6. Limit e-mail communications to business, not the distribution of jokes.

7. Schedule times to read and respond to professional e-mail. Don't allow it to consume your day.

Schedule Time

> *The hub of activity that occurred in the office was a shock. Incessantly ringing phones, people trying to buzz in through security systems, sick kids . . . I have trouble blocking all that out when I need to focus on a task.*
>
> —An elementary principal

Create a personal calendar and time schedule to manage activities. Be aware of any school district office-hour requirements for principals.

The pace of activities and demands increase when students and teachers return. Having systems in place for daily activities will help. Time must be allotted for (a) reading mail, (b) writing correspondence, (c) doing paperwork, (d) answering telephone calls, (e) meeting with visitors, (f) conferring with staff, (g) supervising staff, and (h) attending meetings. Additionally, there will be evening activities and athletic events to attend.

Plan the calendar for the entire year. Record every event and activity that is scheduled on the calendar. Schedule faculty meetings and tentative times for formal classroom observations.

Plan Routine Activities

Schedule daily activities, such as greeting staff and students at the door, monitoring the cafeteria, visiting classrooms, handling correspondence, and answering phone messages. Block out times for meetings and working on long-term goals.

Prioritize Daily Goals

> *I have to work off a priority list. I just can't do it all, all the time, and be everything to everyone.*
>
> —A high school principal

Set goals for each day. Do important things first. If long-range goals are not part of your daily schedule, time will be consumed in putting out fires. Important goals will be ignored. According to one beginning principal, "learning to prioritize" was an important first step.

Each morning tape a list of two or three goals for the day to the desktop. Keep paperwork for one goal at a time on top of the desk. Focus on completing that work. When one goal is completed, check it off and move on to the next goal.

Keep file folders of other current projects inside a desk drawer. One principal shared, "I use four different colored file folders. The files contain work to complete (a) today, (b) by the end of the week, (c) by the end of the month, and (d) long term. Before I leave each day, I look through my folders, update, and reprioritize the work." Other principals rely on their calendars and day planners to track work that needs to be completed. Select a method and stick with it.

Bring Closure to the Day

At the end of the day, clear the desk, except for the calendar and list of priorities for tomorrow. Put today's work in a desk drawer. Review the goals that were accomplished today and reprioritize goals for tomorrow. Check the calendar and plan tomorrow's schedule. This process provides a sense of accomplishment and purpose.

Train the Office Staff

Office staff members who are skilled in human relations as well as effective office procedures are invaluable. Office personnel need to be experts in dealing with the public and providing information. One principal summarized,

The school receptionist solved most minor problems before they ever reached me. She knew how to defuse angry parents, calm upset students, placate frazzled teachers, and still manage to answer the phone before the third ring. She had an encyclopedic knowledge of students, families, and the school's operation. Whenever parents called, she provided relevant family information and the specifics of the problem before connecting me. When unexpected visitors arrived, she stalled them to give me some preparation time.

Another principal reported,

My secretary had an extraordinary command of the English language and a passion for details. Everything that left the office was well written, attractive, and error-free. She maintained a bank of form letters on her computer for almost every occasion. Whenever I needed a letter, she pulled up a form that I could personalize.

Let Office Staff Run the Office

The office staff knows how to run an office; that is their job. The principal's task is to be an instructional leader for the school. A principal who spends the day micromanaging the office will not have time to be a leader.

Telephone Interruptions

The telephone is a useful communication tool for principals. Telephone interruptions should not control the day, however. Tell the secretary your preferences for handling phone calls from parents, staff members, vendors, and family members. What is and who is important enough for an interruption? When is a message sufficient? Designate a time each day to return telephone calls. If possible, return calls the same day. Remember to provide the secretary with names or introduce family members who may call. Teach your children proper etiquette for calling the school.

Visitors

I didn't realize there were so many interruptions, phone calls, or people just wanting a minute.

—An elementary principal

The principalship is a people business. When school is in session, plan to spend time with people. Try to save important paperwork for times when classes are not in session.

Discuss a system with the office staff for handling visitors. Obviously, asking visitors to make appointments is preferred. This allows the principal to schedule time, gather pertinent information, and be better prepared for meetings. Visitors will be assured of the principal's availability and of having the principal's complete attention for a block of time.

When appointments are scheduled, be clear about the timeframe for the meeting. For instance, "I have an hour available next Tuesday, from 2:00 to 3:00 P.M." Keep conversations focused on the issue. To signal the end of the meeting, summarize what was discussed, organize papers, and stand up. If the issue is unresolved, say, "I have another appointment now, but, if you like, we can schedule another meeting to continue our discussion."

People who are angry or distressed about something do not always call for appointments. They show up at the office. If the secretary turns them away because they do not have an appointment, the problem may escalate. If possible, personally acknowledge the visitor and make arrangements to meet as soon as possible. Defusing the situation is critical.

Vendors and sales representatives should be held to appointments. Instruct the office staff on how to politely deter vendors who arrive without appointments. Be prepared for persistence. One principal recalled a determined salesperson who, told she was leaving for a meeting, waited for her by her car.

Secure Cooperation From Maintenance Staff

Ask principals about their most frustrating problems, and many will report difficulties with the custodian. Be sure maintenance personnel are well selected, appropriately trained, and know the importance of their role. Include them in appropriate school discussions, decisions, and celebrations. People who feel part of the team, will work harder.

Organize Paperwork

Principals live in a blizzard of paperwork. If it is not organized, it will be overwhelming.

First, establish a system with the secretary for opening and prioritizing mail. One principal's solution:

> I had my secretary open and file each day's mail into three baskets: one basket for mail that needed my immediate attention; a second basket with mail that should be handled within the next few days; and a third basket for advertisements and other low-priority information. I read the mail in the third basket over a wastebasket.

Second, handle each piece of paper only once. Read it and do something with it: answer it, file it, or throw it away. If it requires a response, make responding as simple as possible. If appropriate, write a response or answer to a question directly on the original and return it to the sender. Make a copy if a record is needed.

Third, for routine correspondence, memos, and reports, create templates using standard phrases. Save the templates on the computer, retrieve, and personalize correspondence for specific use. The time you take to create the templates will pay off again and again. Books, such as Grady's *124 High Impact Letters for Busy Principals* (2001), provide valuable templates for frequent correspondence.

Fourth, categorize and maintain files for routine correspondence that can be used as a reference. Update the files regularly.

Learn to Delegate

Delegating is essential to surviving the principalship. Yet many beginning principals do not delegate duties. One beginner explained, "I was surprised by my inability to delegate. I did my job and everyone else's job. The good people were already busy, and I felt bad giving them more to do. The others, I didn't trust enough to delegate to." The keys to successful delegating include the following:

- Knowing the personnel
- Selecting the correct person
- Providing adequate training, direction, resources, and autonomy
- Monitoring progress

Learn to Say No

I've learned that I'm not superwoman.

—A middle school principal

No principal can do everything and do it well. When asked to do something, consider priorities. Say "yes" to the things that match goals. For other opportunities that do not match goals, be gracious, but firm: "No, I'm over-committed right now, but thank you for the offer."

Plan for Big Projects

A principal's role is fragmented, fast-paced, and fraught with distractions and interruptions. Completing a large-scale or detailed project in a single sitting may be impossible. Instead of being frustrated, create a strategy for completing lengthy paper work. Options include completing paper work before or after school or taking the work home. Now and then it may be necessary to schedule a block of time with the door closed to complete a project. Barricading yourself in the office should be the exception, however, not the rule.

Read Selectively

Principals are deluged with information. Reading all of it is impossible. Yet how do you decide which pieces are important and which to discard? Save time by first scanning the information. Look for key words and phrases. If it appears to have some importance, skim it, noting the publication date, author's credentials, headings, and subtopics. If it begins to look important, preread. Note the thesis statement, opening paragraph, topic sentence in each paragraph, and the summary. Finally, if the information appears to be worthy, deep-read the material, objectively, reflectively, and critically (Mindell, 1993).

Minimize Socializing

Conversing with personnel, visitors, and students is important. Too much socializing, however, can intrude on the time you need for other tasks. Maintain reasonable limits on the time you spend socializing.

Minimize Meetings

If you want to invite two-way communication, hold a meeting. If you want to impart information without inviting input from attendees, send a memo. When you do call a meeting, take steps to make it productive. Suggestions include the following:

- Distribute an agenda before the meeting.
- Establish a reasonable meeting length.
- Notify participants who will be asked to contribute information.
- Adhere to the designated starting time.
- Adhere to the agenda.
- Invite discussion with time limits.
- Adhere to the designated ending time. (Brock & Grady, 2002)

Do What Is Important

> *There's nothing so useless as doing efficiently that which should not be done at all.*
>
> —Peter Drucker

After a few months on the job, assess how you are using your time. First, compile a prioritized list of activities based on their importance. Second, find out how you actually spend your time by keeping a time log for a week. Carry a small notebook with you and record everything you do, the time you begin, and the time you end. At the end of the week, identify the main categories of time expenditures, including the amount of time spent on each. Determine the following:

1. How does the list of priorities compare with the list of actual activities?

2. Which priorities are not being addressed?

3. What activities are time wasters?

4. What activities can or should be omitted?

5. What activities should be delegated?

6. What activities can be accomplished in less time?

7. Which of the following factors are making you feel overworked?

   - A revolving office door
   - Poorly designed work space
   - Lack of organization
   - Cluttered office
   - Lack of clear priorities
   - Inefficient use of time
   - Poorly trained office staff
   - Uncooperative personnel
   - Refusal to delegate
   - Perfectionism
   - Reluctance to share leadership
   - Too many meetings
   - Inability to say no
   - Ineffective people skills. (Brock & Grady, 2002, p. 73)

THE PRINCIPAL'S KEY

All principals lament the lack of time to complete their work. However, effective use of time is a distinguishing characteristic of successful principals. Learn and practice time-management skills so that you can maximize the time you spend at school. Organize the work, establish procedures, and identify a clear focus for the work so that you can achieve your goals.

7 Solve Problems, Dilemmas, and Grievances

Stubbornness should be avoided if one wants cooperation.
—A beginning elementary principal

When you signed the contract, you accepted all the past, present, and future problems of the school. The problems that challenged your predecessor will be waiting for you. In fact, some of them will be standing outside the door when you arrive. As one principal recalled,

> During my first week, a parent complained that a teacher had slapped her child just before school ended in May. Now it was July. I didn't know the teacher, the parent, or the child. In fact, I hardly knew my way around the building. What a way to begin.

TAKE TIME TO THINK

Time is your ally when confronted with a problem. Do not make a hasty decision unless, of course, safety is at stake. Although some problems are important and need resolution, others disappear like the morning dew.

When an issue requires attention, listen carefully to the problem and negotiate for enough time to uncover all the facts and consider the consequences of the decision. A response such as "I will look into this and get back to you tomorrow" tells the person you are interested and plan to address the issue. Provide a timeframe, at least 24 hours, for your response and be sure to follow through. If you do not follow through, you will lose trust and create additional problems.

Dealing With Dilemmas

Trying to solve dilemmas is almost futile. Solutions exist for problems; dilemmas, in contrast, have no clear-cut solutions—only adjustments that make them manageable. For instance, an argument between two students is a problem with a possible solution. Conversely, total elimination of fighting is a dilemma. Although discipline policies, supervision, and teaching students conflict resolution skills may minimize fighting, total elimination of student disputes is unlikely.

Routine Dilemmas

Eventually, dilemmas, because of their repetitious nature, become routine for principals. When they become routine, principals may fail to see opportunities for better resolution of the dilemmas. Dilemmas need to be continually reevaluated.

Some dilemmas, while reoccurring issues for principals, are new and discomforting for parents. For example, entering a child in school, dealing with teenage behavior or testing for learning disabilities are emotionally laden experiences for parents. These issues become routine dilemmas for experienced principals. For individuals experiencing a situation for the first time, the situation is of extreme importance. A principal's blasé attitude toward these issues may appear uncaring. Consider these issues through the eyes of the parents.

One retired elementary principal provided this example:

Every year the same scenario occurred on the first day of school. Two groups of parents formed outside the kindergarten room, one group weeping and clutching their children as though they were going to the gallows—which, of course, made their children cry hysterically. The other group was joyfully contributing to the confusion by recording everything on video camera. Nothing was too insignificant for inclusion. Although the occasion was routine for me, I had to remind myself that it was a milestone in the lives of these children and their parents.

Complaints

Principals spend a significant amount of time listening to complaints and resolving conflicts. Major and minor problems are often described with equal fervor, leaving the principal to determine the validity and importance of each. Active listening is paramount. Listen for emotions and issues that underlie the words being spoken. Clarify your understanding of the problem with the messenger. Think before acting, but do take whatever action is appropriate. Procrastinating or ignoring a problem usually compounds it.

Keep a log of communications that includes complaints, complainants, the date, and the action that you took. A written entry serves as a reminder to act and a record of complaints and responses. Periodic reviews of the communication log may reveal emerging patterns of problems and complainers.

Knowing How to Respond

The first step is determining the reason for the complaint. Listen objectively to the words and emotions of the person.

What does the person want? Sometimes people just want to vent. Rather than advice or a solution, they just want to tell someone. The principal's role in this case is to be an understanding listener. The complaint, however, may include a request for you to take some action. If action is required, consider the following:

Is the complaint supported by fact? Before jumping to the defense of current practices, look objectively at the issue presented from the perspective of the complainer. Perhaps the individual presents a new view worthy of consideration. If the individual's information is incomplete or incorrect, communicate the facts.

Is an unexpressed, but underlying issue, the basis for the complaint? Individuals with personal agendas will be frequent complainers. They are the "squeaky wheels" who want to sway decisions in their favor. A log will help identify the "squeaky wheels." A major mistake is assuming that individuals speak for the majority.

Is the issue something that can be controlled? Principals frequently hear complaints about situations that are beyond their authority. Although sometimes people simply want to vent, at other times they act as though the principal possesses unlimited powers. When this is the case, the parameters of the principal's role and power need to be explained. Consider these examples from one principal's journal:

> Mrs. Jones, I have no control over who drops cigarette butts outside the church next door and no authority to send someone over there to pick them up. A better choice would be teaching Johnny not to pick up the cigarette butts. . . .
>
> I understand that your child's coat was stolen at the public library, but I have no control over security at the library . . . just because the library is across the street from the school doesn't change that . . .

How important is the issue to the school? If the issue is based in fact, is important to the school, and is under the principal's control, it merits consideration and possible intervention. Determine whether the issue is a dilemma or a problem and intervene accordingly.

Pick Your Battles

The principal does not need to address every issue. One principal described learning that lesson during her second year: "I finally trusted others instead of feeling that I had to know everything and make every decision."

Take a stand on issues that are nonnegotiable. Empower others to decide on smaller issues that matter to them or their group. If you do not know an answer or do not have a solution, say so. One principal said, "I overcame my fear of saying, 'I don't know.' When I let my staff see the human side of me, our relationship improved."

Determining which issues are important, which ones to ignore, and what should be delegated is tricky for beginning principals. One principal provided this example: "I made the mistake of meddling in the organization of a faculty social affair. What do I care how a bunch of adults handle a party? My involvement wasn't necessary." Inability to gauge the importance of issues is a common cause of principals' failure. Principals must learn to balance diverse political demands and pressures imposed by members of the school and community. Principals must determine the following:

- How important is the issue?
- Is this a nonnegotiable issue for my administration?
- Who does the issue affect?
- Does the issue affect students and their learning needs?
- Who has greatest expertise in this area?

Student Discipline

Although principals play a major role in establishing a safe and orderly school, they should not accept the role of resident disciplinarian. Principals who accept this role do not have time to pursue school goals. In addition, they unintentionally undermine the authority of the teachers. The principal's role in student discipline is to

- Communicate expectations for appropriate conduct.
- Establish and insist on adherence to school rules.
- Follow district disciplinary codes.
- Support teachers' disciplinary actions.
- Assist teachers in strengthening classroom management skills.
- Enact disciplinary measures for serious student offenses.

Classroom teachers should handle routine disciplinary matters. Only serious infractions should be brought to the attention of the principal. If you succeed a principal who was the "resident disciplinarian," it may take teachers and students time to adjust, as this middle school principal reported, "Initially, the teachers thought I was 'shirking my responsibilities' by not handling all of the discipline. But once they started managing their classrooms better, their problems actually diminished."

When the problem is serious, the principal should be notified. Disciplinary actions taken by the principal should closely adhere to district or school discipline policies and afford due process to the student. As rules of thumb:

1. Diffuse your own emotions.

2. Approach the student objectively.

3. Explain the accusation and supporting facts. Check for understanding.

4. Listen to the student's explanation. Rephrase the student's account and check for understanding.

5. If the student's behavior poses a danger to self or others, follow the measures outlined in your district or school policy. Keep the student under observation until authorities and parents arrive.

6. If the matter is serious but poses no danger, gather all the facts surrounding the situation. Be thorough.

7. Make a decision.

8. Inform student, parents, and classroom teacher of your decision using the format prescribed by district or school policies. Document the incident.

The Hawthorne Effect

Paying attention to a problem can make it better. People feel that you have noted and share the concern. Sometimes attention alone makes others more aware and inadvertently solves or diminishes a problem.

The Chronic Complainer

Frequent visitors may be the chronic complainers. One principal likened them to "gnats." They enjoy conflict. If no conflict exists, they create one. They seldom report specific problems, rather dealing in generalities, innuendoes, and secondhand information. Even your best efforts will not resolve their problems because they do not seek resolution but rather the thrill of causing or fanning the flames of unrest. Like gnats, these individuals tend to swarm, creating a frenzy of unrest in a school.

Ignoring the chronic complainer is tempting, but it is also dangerous. All complaints deserve attention. As in the fable of the child who cried "wolf" too often, sometimes a real problem exists. The principal cannot risk ignoring a real problem. A real "wolf" may be hidden within repeated complaints.

Uncovering the root of the chronic complainer's behavior is another option. The person may be harboring an old grudge, jealousy, or perceived injustice or may simply be seeking attention.

When It Is Not Your Ball, Throw It Back

Principals are obligated to address problems that rightfully belong to the school's administrator. Principals are not responsible, however, for problems that other school personnel are hired to handle. Some parents and teachers may view the principal as the "Great Oz." When problems occur, parents call or drop by to see the principal who is expected to solve every problem.

Beware of slipping into the "Great Oz" role. Those who make the mistake of accepting everyone's problems quickly find themselves overwhelmed. One beginning principal said, "I wanted to make the teacher's job easier, so I took on their problems—tried to fix everything for them. What a mistake that was. I was soon overwhelmed. But when I tried to stop, they became resentful—angry at me."

If individuals throw you a problem that you do not "own," throw it back. Listen and acknowledge the problem. Then ask them how they plan to solve it. Avoid the pitfalls of personally handling all the conflicts and assuming the role of in-house mediator. Instead, teach personnel and students conflict resolution skills so that they can solve their own conflicts (Bulach et al., 1998).

When It Is Your Ball, Run With It

Schools are filled with individuals with different needs and expectations. Sooner or later, needs and expectations are bound to conflict. Conflict and strong emotions are inevitable. Although we cannot eliminate conflict, we can learn how to manage it and negotiate solutions.

Conflict occurs when a disagreement between two parties involves negative overtones and perceptions of incompatible outcomes. Negative emotional states and negative behaviors occur. The principal's responsibility is to find a way to resolve the conflict.

The Dangers of Conflict

Avoidance of conflict is one of the most common mistakes that principals make (Bulach et al., 1998). When conflict is ignored or allowed to continue, differences multiply and intensify, personalities become confused with issues, people take sides, and relationships are destroyed.

The Benefits of Conflict

When handled properly, conflict can be constructive. Although time-consuming for principals, disagreements raise new viewpoints and perspectives, challenge complacency, and can become the impetus for change (Bulach et al., 1998).

The following behaviors have been reported as producing favorable outcomes in conflict resolution:

- Listening
- Gathering information
- Meeting in a neutral area (Zalman & Bryant, 2002)

Principal behaviors likely to lead to unsuccessful outcomes include the following:

- Making assumptions
- Authoritarian decision making
- Inappropriate meeting arrangements (Zalman & Bryant, 2002)

A CONFLICT RESOLUTION MODEL

Most principals adopt an established procedure to manage conflict and negotiate solutions. Using standardized procedures helps the principal focus on the problem instead of the person and ensures that conflicts are handled with uniform fairness.

Effective conflict resolution consists of two basic steps (Katz & Lawyer, 1993).

1. *Defusing Emotion.* Creating constructive emotional states that enable disputing parties to understand their differences and similarities

2. *Negotiation.* Enabling parties to achieve a successful outcome through joint communications and agreement

Defuse Emotion

Most of the time, parents just need to vent. They are relieved when I listen and don't try to navigate the conversation.
—A high school principal

Angry and upset people want someone to listen to their problems. Arguing or trying to reason with them is futile. Instead, assume a calm demeanor. Move slowly and speak in quiet tones. Let them know you want to hear what they have to say.

If the person makes threats or appears out of control, safety is the primary concern. Position yourself out of arms' reach, preferably with a desk or counter between you and the person. Inform the person that you will not tolerate threats or abusive language. If necessary, contact law enforcement officials and school security personnel.

If the person is upset, but not threatening, take the following steps to defuse the emotions:

1. Tell the individual that you want to listen to the problem.

2. Move to a place where you can sit down and visit.

3. Offer refreshments.

4. Listen, without interrupting, to the problem.

5. Ask questions to clarify understanding. If the individual does not object, take notes.

6. Listen for emotions and underlying issues as well as what the person says. Note nonverbal behavior.

7. When the person is calm, repeat the problem for clarification and check for correct understanding.

State Your Views

1. If the complaint is just, admit your error and make amends.

2. If a third party is involved, ask if an attempt has been made to resolve the problem. If not, offer to arrange a meeting. If the complainant wants you involved, mediate a meeting between the individuals.

3. If you do not have all the information, agree to investigate and schedule another meeting.

4. If you know the facts are incorrect, outline the situation as you see it. Identify areas where you agree and disagree.

5. Anticipate a defensive response. Listen and acknowledge views. Resummarize your view.

6. Summarize both sides.

7. If differences are based on beliefs and values, you will not reach an agreement. Agree to disagree. If differences are concrete, move on to negotiation.

Negotiation

1. Identify the interests and reasons for participants' positions.

2. Develop a problem statement. Write it down.

3. Brainstorm options.

4. Evaluate alternatives.

5. Decide on a solution.

6. Develop an action plan.

7. Build in an evaluation process.

8. Express appreciation to the other party for working through the problem with you.

9. If you reach deadlock, try the following suggestions (Katz & Lawyer, 1993):

   - Reidentify the problem.
   - Reexamine it for underlying interests.
   - Sleep on it.
   - Ask for more data.
   - Try out a proposed solution on a temporary basis.

The Principal as Mediator

Principals frequently become mediators in disputes between staff members and parents.

1. The role of a mediator is to listen to each person's story and make certain that combatants know each other's viewpoints.

2. Sum up the main points of each person's concern and check for mutual agreement on the problem.

3. Ask each person what it will take to end the conflict.

4. If the combatants can agree to each other's requirements, the conflict can be ended. If not, negotiations continue. If the parties involved cannot reach an agreement, the mediator encourages combatants to agree to disagree without being disagreeable.

5. Get each of the parties involved to agree that the conflict is over.

6. Document the complaint, the parties involved, and the resolution.

Dealing With Chronically Difficult People

I learned a lesson when I let a parent's anger "get to me." Now I count to 10—sometimes 20 or 50 to regain my composure, remain polite and be a good listener.

—A beginning principal

Do not take others' behavior personally. Their outbursts are not about you. Remain detached from their emotions.

If you anticipate a stressful meeting, plan how you want to behave. Determine the attitude that will best enable you to get along with this person: calm, caring, patient, confident, assertive. Create an internal state that will enable you to respond appropriately (Brinkman & Kirschner, 1994).

THE PRINCIPAL'S KEY

The prevalence of conflict in a principal's work suggests that beginning principals give serious attention to the topic. The suggestions provided in this chapter offer guidance in responding to these situations. By learning to handle conflicts, the principal can succeed in being "part of the solution" rather than being "part of the problem."

8 Make Effective Changes

Present ideas for change only after they're well developed, and use an approach of "what's in it for them."

—An elementary principal

THE CHALLENGES

Most beginning principals have a vision for their school. That vision, however, is based on limited experience as an administrator and a personalized, outsiders' view of what ought to be. Beginning principals lack the contextual vision of the school that can only be acquired through time and inquiry. Consequently, beginning principals must reconstruct their role and readjust their vision as they understand contextual factors (Macmillan, 1998).

One of the frequent reasons that principals do not succeed "is their failure to make decisions that reflect a thorough understanding of school issues, problems and their relative importance" (Davis, 1997, p. 75). According to Bulach and colleagues (1998), new principals often make snap judgments or changes that lack vision for the school. Sometimes they fail because they are sidetracked by politically charged issues and lose sight of issues with long-term implications for the school (Davis, 1997).

Some principals make changes based on their personal comfort level. They make unnecessary changes to mimic what they enjoyed at another school, while they may avoid making needed changes because they lack the skill to do so.

Change should occur based on the needs of the school, not the comfort of the principal. According to one beginning principal, it is the principal's responsibility to acquire the skills and make the change, "Our school was identified as needing reading assistance. I am learning (rapidly) as much as I can about reading incentives and grantwriting. My comfort level is improving as I learn."

Gather the Facts

> *I assessed school needs by using standardized test scores and doing a needs assessment that included feedback from students, staff, and parents.*
>
> —A beginning middle school principal

An early task of beginning principals is to learn as much about the school and its issues as possible. Before considering any changes, investigate every aspect of the school and community. Form a committee of stakeholders, or several committees if the school is large, and investigate the following:

- *Students.* Achievement levels, honors, disciplinary actions, vandalism, violence, enrollment trends, dropouts, and counseling needs

- *Personnel.* Age, experience, training, tenure, turnover, absenteeism, morale, and job satisfaction

- *School Families.* Language, ethnicity, socioeconomic level, school involvement, and school satisfaction

- *School Programs.* Curriculum issues, teaching methods, new programs, and use of school time

- *Resources.* Adequacy and currency of teaching materials and classroom furnishings and sources of funding

- *School Climate.* Health and safety

- *Community.* Population, economics, lifestyles, employment trends, and involvement and satisfaction with the school

Find answers to the following questions:

1. What are the strengths and weaknesses of the school?

2. What improvements are needed?

3. What changes would bring about improvement?

4. What happens if you do nothing?

5. What additional personnel and resources are required?

Consider the Hot Spots

Be aware that "hot spots" sometimes have political implications. Nevertheless, consider the following:

- Who is clamoring for your attention?
- What reoccurring themes are being communicated?
- What signals of dissatisfaction are you receiving?

Be Aware of the Politics

Be aware of the political factions in the school. School politics are complicated. A variety of groups with diverse political agendas compete for time, space, attention, and resources. Teachers, parents, community members, central office staff, and school boards vie for changes that meet their needs. The changes that they want may not be the best choices for the school.

School politics require careful handling. Principals are challenged to effect changes that benefit students and improve learning without alienating politically powerful groups.

Successful principals use political power to their advantage. They find out who wields political power and, whenever possible, enlist those individuals as team players. They do not pick political sides or become embroiled in political power games. They do not make decisions based on "squeaky wheels" or political pressure. Instead, they learn how to lobby and negotiate for what they want. They make decisions that are good for students.

Determine the Problem's Core

Once the problem areas have been identified, determine the core of the problem.

Obvious Needs

Some needs are obvious, such as vacancies, pending litigation, needed repairs, and disgruntled parents. These problems require immediate fact-finding and action. Although a complex problem may be an underlying factor, keep the immediate solution simple. Address the underlying problem after you have acquired all the facts and gained the support of the school community.

Cultural Problems

A school's problems sometimes emerge from the prevailing culture. Entrenched behaviors, although once valued or necessary, may become the source of problems. Uncovering and changing cultural behaviors requires extensive fact-gathering and the cooperation of the entire school community.

Buried Problems

Seemingly superficial yet reoccurring problems may be symptomatic of a deeper problem. Ask why the problem is occurring. Determine if the problem is the real issue or merely a symptom of an underlying problem.

As an outsider, you have the advantage of an unbiased view of the situation; the disadvantage you have is ignorance of extenuating circumstances. Assume nothing. The more information and input that you gather, the better the chances of locating the root of the problem.

Decide Whether Change Is Necessary

If you determine that change is needed, identify possible solutions to the problems. Talk with colleagues and staff members. Review the literature to see how other schools are handling similar issues.

Before proposing any changes, consider the following:

1. What would happen if you did nothing? Is this a situation that will resolve itself?

2. How critical is the need for change? If student learning is impeded or students are endangered, change is imperative.

3. What actions could you take to improve the situation?

4. Do you have the authority to make the change?

5. Have you established the trust necessary to make the change?

6. What are the long-range implications of the change?

7. What and who will block the change?

8. Who will support the change?

9. Who will the change affect?

10. What additional staff, expertise, and resources do you need?

11. How much time will be required?

12. Will the staff require additional training? If so, who will provide it?

13. How will you acquire additional funding or personnel?

14. How will you generate school and community support?

15. Are you prepared to accept the risk?

Planning the Change

Once the decision has been made to risk a change, prepare carefully. First, small but welcome changes should precede any major, potentially unwelcome change. If several major changes are necessary, prioritize them. As one beginning principal suggested, "Prioritize based on the things that matter to people." Determine which change the school will make first. Make sure that a level of trust has been established. Do not proceed without it.

Timing Is Everything

Timing is critical to successful change. New principals need to take time to gather data and establish a team approach to the change. One principal suggested,

> Before I tackled the big problems, I made simple changes that I knew would be successful and popular. I added improvements to the teachers' workroom, cut down on unnecessary meetings, and made simple changes to improve communication with parents. The changes were simple, successful, and popular, consequently paving the way for more complex issues.

How do you know the time is right?

- When the need is present.
- When it is the best thing for the school.
- When doing nothing causes further damage.
- When all the facts are known.
- When trust and approval are high.
- When the personnel and resources are available to make the change.
- When there is a commitment to change.

Initiating the Change

> *Principals need to be meticulous in their preparation, organization, and follow-through.*
> —A middle school principal

Once the change has been identified, establish short- and long-term goals and corresponding strategies. Consider the following:

- Who will be involved in making the change?
- How adequate is the staff?

- Who will the change affect?
- How will those affected respond?
- What materials, equipment, and resources are required?
- What funding source is available?
- What training is needed?
- How much time will the change require?
- How will the change be evaluated?

Handling Opposition

Although a school's constituents may clamor for change, they may not welcome it. They may want certain aspects of the school's program or procedures to change, but they do not want their personal comfort disturbed.

As one principal observed, "The school board demanded that each student who left the school be computer literate. However, when we requested funding for additional computers and software to enhance the program, we were refused."

Another said,

> My first weeks on the job, parents and teachers all complained that student discipline was too lax, that the school discipline code wasn't being enforced. However, when I started enforcing the discipline policy, I discovered that parents wanted other people's kids disciplined, but not their child. Teachers were upset because, unlike my predecessor, I refused to be the resident disciplinarian. Instead, I encouraged them to learn to improve their classroom management skills and refer only major discipline problems to the office.

Change creates anxiety and fear of the unknown. Individually, people fear loss of autonomy, territory, and resources. Collectively, they fear changes in norms. One teacher recalled, "I loved my school until the new principal came and changed the rules. We became a school focused on athletics instead of academics. Honors programs were eliminated. Discipline became lax. I moved to a different school."

Involve Others

You can alleviate some of the anxiety by involving as many people as possible in the change process. Provide ample information about proposed changes. Discuss concerns. If the change involves new procedures, reassure staff that resources and training will be provided.

Share Information

When the plan is launched, provide a copy of it to constituents. Monitor and communicate progress. Celebrate progress and success; encourage participants when setbacks occur. Let participants know that their efforts are appreciated. Provide incentives for cooperation, such as recognition and bonuses.

1. Plan only one major change at a time. Focus energy and attention in one area.

2. Involve the people who will be affected by the change. They need to understand the rationale for change and have input into decisions that will affect them.

3. Appoint respected and expert leaders to assist you.

4. Identify roadblocks and critics. They can sabotage your success. Determine how to remove them, work around them, or use them.

5. Decide on a course of action and market it. Get others interested.

6. Create a plan, a time line, and a budget. Share information so that everyone is moving in the same direction. Do not plan an idea to death. Move on it.

7. Provide any staff training that is required. Fear is dispelled when people feel comfortable with new responsibilities.

8. Assign responsibilities. Include as many people as possible so they have ownership in the change.

9. Implement the plan.

10. Monitor progress. Publicize successes. Reward appropriate behaviors.

11. Evaluate. Few things are perfect the first time. Do not allow minor setbacks to spell defeat.

12. Refine and keep moving.

13. Institutionalize the change. Time and vigilance are required to maintain change and make it part of the school's culture.

Selling Techniques of the Experts

Have you ever purchased something that you did not intend to purchase, did not even know you wanted? If so, you were probably influenced by an expert salesperson.

People who make their living selling products have well-refined strategies for convincing people to buy things. The strategies they use should be considered by principals who want to market ideas.

First, sales experts know that selling something is based on establishing a relationship with the buyer. People are more likely to buy something from a person whom they like and trust. Second, sales experts describe the product and its advantages in language the buyer understands. They focus on the value of the product to the customer, never the cost. Experts move the buyer in well-timed, incremental steps and close the deal with a commitment to purchase. They expect that some buyers will have doubts, questions, and remorse when they get home. Consequently, they are prepared to "resell" the product once the buyer has thought about it.

Principals can learn from the experts and sell their ideas by

1. Establishing trusting relationships.

2. Talking about the proposed change in understandable language.

3. Pointing out the advantages.

4. Focusing on value—never cost.

5. Providing well-timed, incremental information as plans develop.

6. Reselling the proposal many times as questions and doubts arise.

Handling Mistakes

If you fall, pick up something while you're down there.
—New England proverb

Expect to make mistakes. All principals, whether beginners or veterans, make mistakes. It would be ideal to anticipate and avoid every problem; however, this is not realistic.

When mistakes happen, acknowledge them, make corrections, and move forward. Do not exacerbate the situation by sulking or laying the blame elsewhere. As Benjamin Franklin said, "He who is good at making excuses is seldom good at anything else."

Be realistic about the severity of the mistake and adjust your distress level accordingly. Keep things in perspective. If the mistake is serious, ask for help from someone more knowledgeable. If the mistake is minor, have a good laugh.

When a mistake shakes confidence in the school, damage control is necessary. Be honest about what happened. Take responsibility. Show concern. Explain how the problem was or will be resolved. Exude confidence.

Learn from an error so that it is not repeated. Identify what went wrong. Were directions fuzzy? Were expectations unclear? Was supervision adequate? Were the wrong individuals selected for the job? Were resources adequate? Were all consequences and outcomes anticipated? Was timing wrong?

When failures occur, assume responsibility for them. Attributing failure or blaming others is nonproductive and contributes to a climate of fear. Identify the behaviors that contributed to the mistake or failure and change the behavior (Davis, 1997).

THE PRINCIPAL'S KEY

> *The success of the first change you make is critical. If the planning and implementation are successful, faculty and parent leaders will gain trust and confidence in your leadership ability.*
>
> —Brock and Grady (1995, p. 45)

For a beginning principal, the keys to making change are to

- Know the school's strengths, weaknesses, and constraints.
- Determine what needs to be changed and what needs to be left alone.
- Acquire trust.
- Make small, welcome changes before tackling larger, unwelcome ones.
- Pick the right time to initiate major change.
- Involve the people who will be affected.
- Expect tension and apprehension.

9 Take Care of Yourself

The only person over whom you have direct and immediate control is yourself.

—Stephen Covey

Gradually you will begin to feel accepted, know what to anticipate, and have fewer surprises. Tasks that once seemed daunting will no longer be overwhelming. Good days will begin to outnumber bad days.

School improvement is the reflection of leadership. The impact of initiatives that lead to school improvement, however, may not be observed for several years. Not all change efforts will be successful. The relentless pace, heavy workload, uncertainty, and delayed rewards contribute to stress.

LEARN TO MANAGE STRESS

My second year, I was much more relaxed, which in turn, caused people to be relaxed around me.

—A high school principal

How you manage stress will affect your ability to lead as well as your health. Leadership requires energy, stamina, and emotional stability, as well as excellent physical and mental health. Stress can destroy both your health and your career. Stress management is essential to survival as a principal.

Role of Stress

Every activity, pleasurable or not, triggers stress. The joyful anticipation of a vacation, party, or wedding generates stress, as does the dreaded prospect of speaking in public or dealing with an angry parent.

Stress is part of life. Stress is caused by anything that stimulates our attention and is important to us. Without stress, we would not have the interest or motivation to get out of bed in the morning. The principalship includes significant sources of stress.

A Matter of Perception

> *You're nothing but a pack of cards.*
>
> —Alice to the Queen of Hearts in
> Lewis Carroll's *Alice in Wonderland*

Whether an activity or situation is stressful depends on how it is perceived. If the situation is important and the individual feels unsure of the ability to handle it, stress is experienced. As one beginning principal noted, "No one places pressure on me. The pressure is all mine."

An activity that produces stress for one person might be considered routine for another person. Some stress has a positive effect; other stress is negative.

How Much Is Too Much?

People have varying degrees of stress tolerance. What is normal stress to one person is overwhelming distress to another. Signs of too much stress include restless sleep or sleeplessness, fatigue, illness, feeling overwhelmed, lack of enjoyment of pleasurable activities, and loss of emotional control.

Capitalizing on Stress

Although principals can do little to decrease the stress in their role, they can learn to manage and capitalize on that stress. Some principals appear to thrive on stress, but others succumb to its negative effects. How an individual chooses to perceive and manage stress is the difference.

WHAT TRIGGERS STRESS?

Stress occurs at the intersection of personality traits combined with personal and workplace issues. Examining each of these components will reveal your personal stress triggers.

Some individuals possess personalities that increase their proclivity to stress. Factors include self-concept, perfectionism, personality type, and locus of control.

Self-Concept

Do you have low self-esteem? Individuals with low self-esteem may succumb to the emotional pressures of the principal's role. The demands of the work are overwhelming and emotionally exhausting. They feel unable to live up to others' expectations and standards, thereby reinforcing their feelings of low self-esteem.

Perfectionism

Do you feel that you must do everything perfectly? Are you unable to trust anyone else to do the job as well as you? If so, you may soon be feeling the enormous pressure of being overworked.

Personality Traits

Do you have a Type A personality? If you are always in a hurry, impatient, competitive, and have high expectations, you may have a Type A personality. People with this personality type are compulsive overachievers who set unrealistic expectations and heavy workloads for themselves. They wait until the last minute to complete work, excusing their procrastination with "I work better under pressure." Last minute deadlines create undue stress for them and the people with whom they work.

If you have a Type B personality, you are more relaxed in your approach to life and work and consequently experience less stress. You have a more balanced approach, selecting projects that fit within your goals and that can be reasonably completed in the time allowed. You plan ahead to complete work well before deadlines.

Locus of Control

Do you believe that you are in control of circumstances in your work, or do you feel controlled by circumstances in your work? People who feel in control have an internal locus of control and suffer less stress. Those who feel out of control have an external locus of control and experience greater stress.

Gender

Are you the primary caretaker of a home, young children, or aging parents? Female administrators often experience added stress due to the comingled responsibilities of career, household tasks, and caring for family members. In spite of changing societal norms, women are often considered the primary caretakers of home and children. Men in dual-career marriages may also experience pressure to contribute to household tasks and child care, however. Additionally, principals who belong to the "stretch generation" often have dual responsibilities for raising children and caring for elderly parents.

Ethnicity

Are you a minority in your workplace? Ethnic origins may contribute to tensions. Principals who belong to a minority group may be scrutinized, have their competence challenged, or be resented because they were selected.

Personal Issues

Do you have personal problems? Personal circumstances may exacerbate already stressful work situations. Problems from home seldom stay there. Instead they follow us to work and combine with the stresses of the job.

Personal issues that trigger stress include the following (Brock & Grady, 2002, p. 18):

- Raising children and running a home while working full time (If you are a single parent, the burden increases.)
- Caring for aging parents
- Dealing with personal or a family member's illness
- Dealing with a chemically dependent family member
- Extreme behavior problems of a child
- Birth or adoption of a child
- Marital problems or divorce
- A new marriage
- Financial problems
- Recent death in the family
- Moving to a different home
- Remodeling a home
- A child leaving home

The Workplace

What causes you the most stress at work? You can probably identify factors common to most principals. They include the following (Gmelch & Torelli, 1994):

- *Role-Based Stress.* Your role is not clearly defined or you are given competing roles or incompatible directives.

- *Daily Activities.* Daily activities on the job cause stress.
- *Boundary-Spanning Stress.* External issues, student's parents, or community groups cause stress.
- *Conflicts.* Conflicts between individuals or parties cause stress.

SELECT APPROPRIATE RESPONSES

Once the triggers of stress are known, measures to minimize it can be taken. The choice of strategies includes some temporary—and often destructive—responses, as well as others that lead to lifestyle changes.

Negative Responses to Stress

Faced with stress, the normal intent is to restore equilibrium as quickly as possible. Quick fixes, such as sugary treats, chips, tobacco, alcoholic beverages, or drugs are common choices. These are temporary solutions since after the chips are eaten and the beer consumed, the problem that caused the stress remains. Additionally, continual use of food, alcohol, tobacco, and drugs to relieve stress is potentially habit-forming and may create long-term health problems.

Positive Responses to Stress

Better choices for stress management include (a) identifying goals, (b) adjusting attitudes, (c) changing perspectives, or (d) removing stressful circumstances. Sometimes stress is self-imposed. Before blaming an external circumstance or someone else for your stress, first examine yourself.

Identify Goals

Go confidently in the direction of your dreams. Live the life you've imagined.
—Henry David Thoreau

What are your goals for the future? Picture the ideal personal and professional life, and write it down. Be sure that the goals are yours alone and not those that someone else set for you. Self-knowledge and goals are essential to making decisions. If you are out of touch with yourself, you may select inappropriate career moves and life choices. Once you know your desired destination, create an action plan to take you there.

Modify Personality Traits

How much of your stress is due to your personality? Examine your personality to determine how much stress is self-imposed. Some personality traits and their corresponding behaviors thwart progress and create stress. Consider the following: locus of control, perfectionism, attitudes, and perspectives.

Locus of Control

People who fail grasp onto excuses while successful people find a way.
—Richard Geno

Are you in charge of or a victim of your life circumstances? Individuals who believe that circumstances control their lives feel helpless, frustrated, out of control, and stressed. Their attitude is "I can't do it because. . . ." Individuals who are in charge of their circumstances experience less stress. They see challenges where others see constraints and impediments. Their attitude is "I can do it in spite of. . . ."

Perfectionism

Do you need everything to be perfect? Perfectionists are afraid to make mistakes. They spend inordinate amounts of time and energy on projects that are unworthy of the effort. They refuse to delegate, fearing that the work will not meet their standards. Perfectionism leads to stress and exhaustion. Delegating work and assigning time limits for paperwork are helpful strategies.

Overachiever

Are you always rushing, impatient and doing two things at once? Individuals with Type A personalities create stress for themselves and everyone around them. Serenity arrives at the moment you realize that (a) you cannot control everything and (b) some things just are not that important.

Helpful strategies for Type A personalities include the following (Brock & Grady, 2002, p. 12):

- Ignoring the unimportant
- Assigning less importance to events
- Distancing yourself from the problem
- Controlling emotions
- Applying sound problem-solving strategies
- Allowing others to help

RESTRUCTURE YOUR THINKING

How you think affects how you feel and what you do. By changing the way you think, you can change your attitudes, the way you behave, and how others respond to you. By restructuring the way you think, you can decrease stress.

Attitude Is a Choice

Attitudes reflect perceptions of the world and influence responses to events. By controlling attitudes, you can control responses to situations, thereby influencing outcomes. Consider the following situation.

Mark was frustrated and annoyed with Mrs. Smith's repeated complaints. According to her, something or somebody was always causing distress for her child. Now she is back, waiting to speak with him. He has two choices. He can allow his negative attitude to dictate his behavior, or he can choose to remain positive and keep an open mind. His choice of attitudes and behaviors will influence the outcome of the meeting.

Assigning Power

You have the power to control stress by controlling the amount of power assigned to events. The amount of stress that one feels is proportional to the importance assigned to an event. If the event is perceived as very important, stress occurs. If the event is perceived as unimportant, little stress occurs.

Discard Trivial Stressors

Another way to decrease stress is to stop fretting about insignificant issues. Worrying and fretting about insignificant issues diverts time and attention from that which is important. List the issues that cause stress. How many of them are worthy of the power assigned to them?

A common trivial stressor is the "injured party syndrome." Harboring injustices wastes time and energy. Move on. Do not be controlled by a person or event.

Control Worrying

Abraham Lincoln told the story of an Eastern monarch who charged his wise men to invent a sentence that would be true and appropriate at all times and situations. They presented him with the words, "And this, too, shall pass."

Worrying is a major waste of time. How many of the situations you worried about last week, month, or year happened?

Relieve stress by mentally distancing yourself from problems. Use cognitive restructuring to change perspectives. Consider the problem as though it belonged to someone else. How important is this problem? Will it be important to anyone next week, month, or year? What's the worst possible outcome and how likely is that to occur? How long will the situation last? How can I resolve the problem (Brock & Grady, 2002)?

One beginning principal, feeling overwhelmed by the workload, described how she avoided worrying about it:

> One night I made a long list and prioritized the things I needed to accomplish according to tomorrow, soonest, delay. I estimated the amount of time I needed for each task. The process helped me break my workload into manageable parts and go to sleep without all of it dancing in my head.

Control Your Emotions

You cannot fix a damaged watch with a hammer.
—M. R. Kopmeyer

When a parent with an unsubstantiated complaint visits for the third time in a week, it is natural to feel annoyance, even anger. Responding emotionally is not the best choice. Instead, separate emotions from the situation and plan how to respond. Breathe deeply, compose yourself. Gather all the facts and remember that this is not a personal issue, but a difference of opinion. After the meeting, vent your emotions in an acceptable setting.

Stockpiled emotions tend to erupt and splash on unfortunate bystanders, usually staff and family members. Loss of emotional control contributes to damaged relationships. Instead of stockpiling, find ways to release emotions in acceptable ways throughout the day.

Think Positively

When problems occur, it is easy to become overwhelmed, to lose perspective, and to feel unsuccessful. When you feel discouraged, consider current problems in the context of past successes. Principals use a variety of techniques to maintain a positive focus. Some principals keep journals of their experiences, lists of accomplishments, and folders of thank-you notes. Reflect on past successes. One principal had help from her secretary, "Whenever I was in the doldrums, my secretary would begin listing the positive changes that I had made in the school. She helped me put problems in perspective."

Take Risks

If you follow the crowd, the only place it will lead you to is the exit.
—Robin Sharma

Think new thoughts. Have the courage to try new ideas. Managers maintain what exists, but leaders create something better. Abandon the herd and become a creative leader.

Visualize Success

When you plan to face a difficult situation, rehearse it in your imagination. Picture the setting, how you will behave, and what you will say. Imagine a successful conclusion or result.

TAKE CARE OF YOUR HEALTH

Beginning administrators are vulnerable to stress-related health problems. Schmidt and colleagues (1998a) reported that beginning principals of both genders, "with African Americans and females most affected, became more controlled, exacting, tense, driven, and overwrought" (p. 11). In another report, they noted that blood pressure increased for male African American principals and female principals during the first three years of their principalship (Schmidt, Kosmoski, & Pollack, 1998b). Given the vulnerability of novice principals to stress-related health risks, proactive safeguarding of physical, emotional, and spiritual health is critical.

Physical Health

Care for yourself before attempting to care for another. The old saying "You have everything if you have your health" is true. Good health is a valuable resource. Once lost or damaged, it is difficult, and sometimes impossible, to regain.

Positive health practices include the following:

- Regular checkups
- Regular exercise
- Adequate rest
- Dietary monitoring
- Stress-reduction techniques
- Judicious use of alcohol
- Not smoking

Spiritual Health

Spiritually healthy people have a sense of inner calm and peace. They give of themselves, but also replenish themselves spiritually by spending time alone each day. Solitude rests the spirit, refreshes the soul, and reenergizes creativity.

Time spent each day in solitude is essential to inner harmony. Relaxing activities vary according to individual interests. Suggested activities include the following:

- Reading
- Playing with a pet
- Running
- Biking
- Playing the piano
- Gardening
- Painting
- Cooking
- Building
- Collecting
- Riding a horse
- Hiking
- Gardening

Play more. Mimic children and nourish yourself with play. Find a personal solution that rejuvenates your spirit and make it part of a regular routine.

FIND A BALANCE

Although a principal's work is important, it constitutes only one part of a life. There is more to life than a job. A balanced life includes friends, family, and outside interests. Spend time with people you enjoy. Friends help you maintain perspective.

Develop the ability to laugh at yourself. The predicaments of a school day can provide fodder for humor for many months and years. Look for the lighter side of dilemmas. Keep a journal of the funny things that occur.

One principal remarked on the value of her "eternal optimism and smile." Smile at people. They smile back.

CONTINUE LEARNING

Assume responsibility for your professional development. Let your supervisor know about your professional growth plan. Your supervisor may be able to provide valuable assistance and resources. Read the books identified in Resource E, which are focused on issues that are critical for beginning principals.

Identify a Role Model

Most successful principals can identify an admired person who served as their leadership model (Osterman & Sullivan, 1996). Select a competent person whose values you respect and identify which behaviors and strategies make them effective. Adopt those behaviors and strategies that are compatible with your personal style and beliefs.

Find a Mentor

If your school district does not provide mentors, find your own. Select a person who is experienced and competent and with whom you feel comfortable. Visit with and enlist the advice of colleagues in the district. Meet with other beginning principals to discuss common problems and solutions.

Network

Become involved in professional organizations, attend conferences and workshops, take classes, and network with others. One rural principal reported, "I started an elementary principals' group within my area. We meet once a month for lunch and share ideas, questions, and concerns. It's been a great support."

Obtain Feedback on Your Performance

Do not assume that you are doing a good job. Determine how teachers and parents perceive your leadership. Use feedback to identify weaknesses. A survey can provide information for improving performance. Invite a colleague to shadow you and share observations afterward.

Look for Indicators to Measure Your Leadership

Increases in complaints, student transfers, or teacher attrition may indicate political problems or inadequate interpersonal skills. Declines in student academic performance may indicate inappropriate decisions in areas such as curriculum, instruction, classroom management, or school safety (Davis, 1997). Student learning is a measure of the principal's effectiveness.

THE PRINCIPAL'S KEY

What would have made my first year easier? Roller skates!
—An elementary principal

The first year as a principal is challenging, sometimes overwhelming, and often exhausting. Yet the voices of first-year principals attest to the rewards of the position.

The principalship is a great profession. I love my job. The kids are great. I love it when they want to share their excitement or beg to show me what they are working on for their classes. I feel honored when they want to share a problem and proud when they show improvement.

Connecting with teachers is enriching. Principals play an important role in their lives. We're the people they introduce to their families and with whom they discuss new ideas and share excitement when babies arrive. It's awesome to be such a positive force in people's lives.

Working with, providing support for, and understanding parents is rewarding.

The bottom line is . . . choose a positive attitude. When you feel like you will never be above water again, kick really hard to get to the top and look around. The positives around you always outweigh the negatives. Focus on those positives.

I am excited and grateful to have such a wonderful opportunity. I enjoy looking at education from a larger viewpoint and having increased adult contact . . . more than I anticipated. I've also discovered some skills that I took for granted.

It's difficult to meet the increasing needs with less money available. Budget became a reality! But I feel confident that I am able to handle what comes my way. My organizational skills have helped me juggle many duties and I am continuously learning and honing my leadership skills.

I feel ready to take on whatever comes in my direction. My family has been awesome . . . their support and understanding have been critical to my success.

I'm beginning to understand how many people it takes to serve the needs of kids. It does indeed "take a village."

The principalship isn't as hard as I thought. I've discovered that I can do it!

The principalship is definitely "worth doing." With proper planning, it can be done very well.

Resource A

School and Self-Assessment Tools

PRINCIPAL'S SCHOOL AND SELF ASSESSMENT

Directions

For use as a self-appraisal tool, identify your personal strengths and weaknesses by answering each question honestly. Checkmarks in the "No" or "Don't Know" column identify areas for improvement.

Do the teachers in my school feel that they	Yes	No	Don't Know
Make a contribution	____	____	____
Have a sense of self-direction	____	____	____
Belong to something	____	____	____
Are part of something important	____	____	____
Know where they fit in	____	____	____
Are competent/successful in one area	____	____	____
Can act independently	____	____	____
May select options or alternatives	____	____	____
Have valued opinions	____	____	____
Have choices	____	____	____
Are cared for as individuals	____	____	____

Do teachers have	Yes	No	Don't Know
Adequate resources	____	____	____
A clean building	____	____	____
An orderly environment	____	____	____
Personal safety	____	____	____
Collegiality	____	____	____
Time to teach	____	____	____
Time for planning	____	____	____

Do I	Yes	No	Don't Know
Focus on individuals	____	____	____
Look for strengths	____	____	____
Place teachers in settings appropriate for their talents	____	____	____
Allow mistakes	____	____	____
Value input	____	____	____
Listen	____	____	____
Assist teachers to maximize their potential	____	____	____
Support their decisions	____	____	____
Make teachers feel good about themselves	____	____	____
Encourage new ideas	____	____	____
Provide recognition	____	____	____

Am I	Yes	No	Don't Know
Cheerful	____	____	____
Optimistic	____	____	____
Respectful	____	____	____
Honest	____	____	____
Trustworthy	____	____	____
Reliable	____	____	____
Decisive	____	____	____
Fair	____	____	____
Helpful	____	____	____
Knowledgeable	____	____	____
Current	____	____	____
Participatory	____	____	____
Welcoming	____	____	____
Open	____	____	____
Flexible	____	____	____
Adaptable	____	____	____
Expert	____	____	____
Collaborative	____	____	____

Accessible	____	____	____
Encouraging	____	____	____
Creative	____	____	____
Enthusiastic	____	____	____

SOURCE: Brock and Grady, (2000). *Rekindling the Flame,* pp. 117–118.

TEACHER'S SCHOOL AND SELF-ASSESSMENT TABLE

Directions

I would like your help in improving our school. Your confidential and anonymous responses to this survey will provide valuable information about how we might make our school an even better place for teachers to work and students to learn.

A summary of all responses will be prepared, and together we will be able to develop plans based on the responses.

Indicate your agreement with the items according to the following scale:

SA = Strongly agree

A = Agree

N = Neither agree nor disagree

D = Disagree

SD = Strongly disagree

	SA	A	N	D	SD
I believe that the quality of my teaching has a definite impact on the success of my school.	——	——	——	——	——
I understand how I contribute to the school's mission.	——	——	——	——	——
As a faculty, we regularly review our progress toward school goals.	——	——	——	——	——
The school district's vision provides a clear direction for the future.	——	——	——	——	——
The faculty is guided by a sense of the school's shared vision and values.	——	——	——	——	——
My school welcomes parent involvement in children's learning.	——	——	——	——	——
My school listens to parents' concerns.	——	——	——	——	——
My school makes student learning a top priority.	——	——	——	——	——

	SA	A	N	D	SD
Our school responds quickly and appropriately to parental feedback.	___	___	___	___	___
All teachers understand the school's policies and procedures.	___	___	___	___	___
I have the resources (materials and equipment) to do quality teaching.	___	___	___	___	___
My workload does not affect the quality of my teaching.	___	___	___	___	___
I am encouraged to actively participate in solving school problems.	___	___	___	___	___
Teachers communicate openly in the school.	___	___	___	___	___
I receive the information I need regarding school affairs and activities.	___	___	___	___	___
Our administrator does a good job of communicating school decisions.	___	___	___	___	___
I have trust in the information that I receive from school administrators.	___	___	___	___	___
I have the freedom I need to use my own judgment in teaching.	___	___	___	___	___
We practice teamwork in our school.	___	___	___	___	___
There is good cooperation between teachers in the school.	___	___	___	___	___
Orientation and induction for new teachers is effective.	___	___	___	___	___
I benefited from the assistance of a mentor during my first year.	___	___	___	___	___
My present assignment provides an opportunity to develop my talents.	___	___	___	___	___
My principal encourages me to develop my teaching ability.	___	___	___	___	___
I know what is expected of me regarding my teaching performance.	___	___	___	___	___
I receive adequate feedback on my performance.	___	___	___	___	___

	SA	A	N	D	SD
I have recently received praise for good work.	___	___	___	___	___
My performance is measured against clearly defined expectations.	___	___	___	___	___
My school uses a fair evaluation system.	___	___	___	___	___
My school celebrates its successes.	___	___	___	___	___
My school recognizes teacher success and achievements.	___	___	___	___	___
My school recognizes student achievement and successes.	___	___	___	___	___
I feel that I have opportunities to develop professionally at my school.	___	___	___	___	___
I am compensated fairly for my work.	___	___	___	___	___
Compared with other schools, my salary is competitive.	___	___	___	___	___
I am satisfied with the benefits provided by my school.	___	___	___	___	___
Information about school and district benefits is clearly communicated.	___	___	___	___	___
My principal treats me with respect.	___	___	___	___	___
My principal responds to my requests for assistance.	___	___	___	___	___
My principal values my ideas.	___	___	___	___	___
My principal encourages me to do high-quality teaching.	___	___	___	___	___
My principal will stand up for me.	___	___	___	___	___
My principal cares about me as a person.	___	___	___	___	___
My principal follows through on commitments.	___	___	___	___	___
My principal treats all personnel fairly.	___	___	___	___	___
We have fun while getting the job done.	___	___	___	___	___

	SA	A	N	D	SD
I have made friendships at school.	____	____	____	____	____
I am able to adjust work hours when needed to meet personal needs.	____	____	____	____	____
My principal recognizes the importance of my personal life.	____	____	____	____	____
My principal takes an interest in the well-being of the staff.	____	____	____	____	____
I like teaching at this school.	____	____	____	____	____
The physical working conditions at my school are good.	____	____	____	____	____
I believe that policies are administered fairly.	____	____	____	____	____
I am satisfied with my job.	____	____	____	____	____
My present assignment provides opportunities to use my talents and skills.	____	____	____	____	____
The morale in the school is good.	____	____	____	____	____
I am proud to work at my school.	____	____	____	____	____
I am optimistic about the future success of this school.	____	____	____	____	____
I can achieve my career goals while working at this school.	____	____	____	____	____
I would encourage my friends to teach at this school.	____	____	____	____	____
I plan to teach at this school for many years.	____	____	____	____	____

SOURCE: Brock & Grady, 2000, *Rekindling the Flame: A Guide for Beginning Principals,* pp. 119–120.

Resource B

Your Educational Philosophy

Directions

Write your educational philosophy by completing the following sentences.

1. The purpose of education is _____
   _____
   _____
   _____
   _____
   _____
   _____
   _____
   _____
   _____

2. A good education includes _____
   _____
   _____
   _____
   _____
   _____
   _____
   _____
   _____
   _____

3. All people deserve to be treated _____

_____
_____
_____
_____
_____
_____
_____
_____

4. I have the following core (nonnegotiable) values: _____

_____
_____
_____
_____
_____
_____
_____
_____

5. The role of the principal is _____

_____
_____
_____
_____
_____
_____
_____
_____

6. The role of the teacher is _____

_____
_____
_____
_____
_____
_____
_____
_____

7. The role of the student is _____
   _____
   _____
   _____
   _____
   _____
   _____
   _____
   _____

8. The role of parents is _____
   _____
   _____
   _____
   _____
   _____
   _____
   _____
   _____

9. The role of the community is _____
   _____
   _____
   _____
   _____
   _____
   _____
   _____
   _____

10. I want this school to become _____
    _____
    _____
    _____
    _____
    _____
    _____
    _____
    _____

11. I want others to perceive me as _____

_____

_____

_____

_____

_____

_____

12. I will know that students are learning when _____

_____

_____

_____

_____

_____

_____

Resource C

The Job Selection Process

Examining Potential Matches

If you are considering applying for a principalship position, these are questions and issues to consider.

DO YOUR HOMEWORK

Before applying for a position, investigate the school district, community, and school setting. Match your personality, experiences, background, and career goals with a position that will allow you to succeed.

Principals who accept the first job offered to them may find themselves in work settings that are incongruous with their philosophy, values, skills, and background. Aspiring principals may assume that if they do not like a position, they will simply move on to another position. Leaving an ill-suited principalship, however, can create another set of problems. First, finding another position takes time. Second, hiring authorities may look unfavorably at individuals who have short tenures at previous positions. Third, obtaining favorable recommendations may be a problem. Fourth, a principal in an ill-suited position risks termination, which can destroy a promising career.

Gather information about the school and district from available written documents that describe the school, district, and community, including principal job descriptions, mission statements, handbooks, curriculum guides, standardized test scores, and annual reports. The state department of education can provide demographic information about the school and district. This information may be available on the school district's and the department of education's Web sites.

The written information reveals the prescriptive culture of a district—the vision to which the district aspires. The descriptive culture, or that which routinely happens in the district, may be different. Past and present employees, businesspeople, parents, students, and newspaper articles are important sources of information about daily life at the school.

The Predecessors

Find out why the position is available. Learn as much as you can about the previous principals, particularly information about length of tenure and reasons for leaving. What is the turnover rate of principals and teachers at the school? If the turnover rate has been frequent, what is the reason? Consider the risks if you take the position.

If leadership changes have been frequent, teachers may be distrustful, unwilling to make changes. Others will welcome another opportunity for stability. In the absence of formal leadership continuity, informal leaders may have emerged from the faculty who will resist interference from the new principal.

If the predecessor's tenure was lengthy and uneventful, teachers may resist innovation and change. Others will welcome the opportunity to make improvements.

The loss of a beloved or charismatic principal, through death, transfer, or retirement, can be problematic. School communities will mourn the loss, sometimes to the degree of idealizing the person. Meanwhile, the new principal is considered an unwelcome, ineffective substitute. Mourning periods may last for a long time.

Forced successions, such as terminations, may inspire resentment, while legitimate factors, such as death, promotion, or retirement may provide a positive environment for a new principal. Promotions may be viewed as signals that the district is pleased with the status quo. Consequently, the successor may feel reluctant to make changes.

The Superintendent

What is the philosophy and leadership style of the superintendent? How does the superintendent communicate with and delegate authority to building principals? What do other principals report about the level of support they receive from the superintendent? How and by whom are principals evaluated?

Expectations

Know the expectations of the district, personnel, and parents before accepting a position. Although their expectations will differ to some extent, be sure that they are compatible. If they are not, you will be caught in a vortex of conflict.

District Expectations

What administrative responsibilities are assigned to the building principal? Consider issues such as obligatory meetings, personnel obligations (recruiting, selecting, supervising, assigning staff), purchasing, budgeting, maintaining financial records, curriculum design, staff development, and involvement in new construction or remodeling. Is the principal responsible for programs such as transportation, athletics, or extended care? Does the principal supervise the cafeteria, custodial, and transportation staff?

Visit the school. Note the condition of the building. Is there a long-range plan for maintenance?

Expectations of Personnel

Knowing the expectations of the teachers and nonprofessional staff is important. They generally accept a principal's leadership when they feel their expectations are being met. When expectations are not met, they will reject your leadership unless you can convince them to modify their expectations.

Expectations of Parents

Parents have expectations for principals based on their perception of a principal's role, the school's needs, and past educational experiences. Their comments will reveal their expectations for the principal. Are they lobbying for school changes?

The Community

Gather information about the people who live in the community. These are the people the school depends on for financial and social support. What makes this community unique? What percentage of the population has school-age children? How economically stable is the community? Are the residents satisfied or dissatisfied with the school? How will you fit into the culture and norms of the community?

The School Staff

The people who work in the school are essential to its success. What are their levels of experience, expertise, and maturity? What is the turnover rate? What is their reputation in the community?

Is there an administrative team? If so, are any members of the team seeking the principal's position? Consider how that will impact your working relationship if you are awarded the position.

Does the school have an effective office, maintenance, custodial, and cafeteria staff?

The Students

The school exists to serve the needs of the students. Consider the following issues to determine if you are prepared to meet their needs:

Enrollment, standardized test scores, culture, primary language, and percentage of special education, gifted, and ESL-ELL students. Does the school have a reputation for excellence in a specific area? If so, are you knowledgeable in the curriculum area? What is the school's reputation for discipline? If a specific discipline model is used, are you knowledgeable about that model?

Resource D

The Interview Process

Tips to Guide You

Issues to consider before interviewing for a position.

THE DUAL PURPOSE OF INTERVIEWS

The purpose of an interview is twofold: first, to determine if the position is suitable for you; second, to determine if you are suitable for the position. In preparation for the interview, consider what additional information you need to made a decision and what the interviewers need to know about you.

Before the interview, clarify your values and your determine your stance on education issues. Decide which values are nonnegotiable. Tell the interviewers who you are rather than what you think they want to hear. Focus on determining if the job and you are a suitable match. Doing otherwise may result in a job in which personal beliefs and values conflict with role. Internal dissonance creates stress and unhappiness and results in ineffective leadership.

The Selection Process

Examine the selection process. Find out about the members of the interview team—their backgrounds, experience, and reputations. If the members of the selection team are held in high regard, their choice of principal will be more highly regarded. If their decisions are not valued, the new leader may struggle to establish credibility.

How large is the pool of candidates? If the pool of candidates is large and the requirements rigorous, you are more likely to be regarded as the best choice. Are candidates being sought from within or outside the organization? If the committee is looking for an outsider, chances are they seek major change. When committees look within the organization, they may seek to maintain existing conditions with only minor changes.

If you are from outside the school district, you may struggle to be accepted, and changes you make will be regarded with skepticism and resistance. What you deem important will be conveyed by what you pay attention to and reward. Staff members and parents will examine, question, scrutinize, and review your words and deeds with skepticism. Your consistency will be monitored.

One principal recalled,

> I sent a note home regarding a new policy on field trips—one that offered greater safety measures for the children. I anticipated little to no reaction. Parents, however, scrutinized and questioned every sentence. Several looked for nonexistent motives for my actions. Some refused to allow their children to participate in field trips for the first semester.

Insiders have the advantage of already knowing the culture and district procedures, but they must also deal with insider politics, jealousy, and old loyalties.

How to Prepare

Learn everything you can about the school, school district, and community. The information you gather will enable you to decide whether this is an appropriate career move for you and, should you decide to pursue to position, to be well prepared for the interview.

The employers are not looking for just any principal; they are looking for a principal who can fill the needs of a specific school setting. The more you know about the setting, the better equipped you will be to anticipate and answer the interviewers' questions.

What to Expect

Search committees vary according to the nature of the school. Generally, they comprise several people, including administrators, teachers, parents, and sometimes students. Sometimes candidates will be invited to a series of interviews.

Prepare for the Interview

Prepare yourself for the interview by clarifying your values and your stance on current educational issues. Interviewers will also want to know why you want to be a principal and why specifically at this school. Prepare yourself in advance by thinking through possible questions and responses based on these factors:

- Your vision
- Your values
- Your skills
- Your experiences
- Your educational background
- Your enthusiasm for the job
- What you will bring to the school
- What will make you an effective leader
- Your leadership style
- Your strongest attributes
- Past successes
- What you have learned from past failures
- Your long-range career plans

The Interview

The interviewers are looking for a person who is passionate about education, who communicates well, and who exudes a calm, confident demeanor. Early impressions count. Arrive on time, smile, introduce yourself to everyone, and shake hands. Throughout the interview, look, behave, and speak like a leader.

During the interview, listen carefully to the questions, look at the speaker, and watch for nonverbal cues. When you respond, show your enthusiasm and personality. Address your answer to everyone in the room. Speak clearly, concisely, and naturally. Make your answers believable. Do not recite answers that sound like passages from a textbook.

Questions

Plan on being invited to ask questions. Have one or two questions prepared in advance, but use them only if that information has not been provided during the interview. Make the questions a natural outgrowth of the interview, for instance, "I understand that the district is considering a new faculty development plan. What direction do you see that plan taking? Your questions provide an opportunity to reinforce your interest in the position and your potential as an effective leader. Additionally, questions enable you to find out information that may be vital to your decision. Do not waste the opportunity by inquiring about the projected time line for a hiring decision. However, do not overextend the interview by asking too many questions. Watch for nonverbal cues that signal the end of the interview.

The Job Offer

Once you sign the administrator's contract, you have accepted the people, issues, and problems that constitute the position. Before you hastily accept, be certain that the position is appropriate for you. If you did your homework and listened carefully during the interview, you will be able to make an informed decision. Consider the following factors:

- Did members of the interview team express congruent values?
- Did they share the same vision and sense of direction?
- Did their responses match the information you learned from talking with community residents, parents, and school employees?
- Are you in agreement with the district's mission, goals, and values?
- Are you and the school's culture a comfortable fit?
- Will you be accepted?
- Are expectations for principals reasonable and doable?
- What is the scope of the principal's authority?
- What is the decision-making process?
- How open are the lines of communication?
- How much support can you expect?
- What specific problems exist in the school?
- Are any legal issues pending?
- What are the expectations for change?
- What disagreements or volatility surround the proposed change?
- Do you have the skill to carry out the changes?
- Are adequate resources available?

Resource E

Annotated Bibliography for Beginning Principals

Borisoff, D., & Victor, D. A. (1998). *Conflict management: A communications skill approach* (2nd ed.). Boston: Allyn & Bacon.

> An intensive examination of language, gender, and cultural factors in conflict.

Brinkman, R., & Kirschner, R. (1994). *Dealing with people you can't stand: How to bring out the best in people at their worst.* New York: McGraw-Hill.

> Practical suggestions for dealing with difficult personalities.

Grady, M. (2001). *124 high-impact letters for busy principals.* Thousand Oaks, CA: Corwin Press.

> A treasury of both routine and hard-to-write sample letters; a CD-ROM is available.

Katz, N. H., & Lawyer, J. W. (1993). *Conflict resolution: Building bridges.* Thousand Oaks, CA: Corwin Press.

> A short, easy-to-read book that provides a practical model of conflict management and resolution.

Ramsey, R. D. (1999). *Lead, follow, or get out of the way.* Thousand Oaks, CA: Corwin Press.

> Practical tips on using leadership tools—speaking, writing, politics, time management, and presenting the image of a leader.

Ricken, R., Terc, M., & Ayres, I. (2001). *The elementary school principal's calendar.* Thousand Oaks, CA: Corwin Press.

> Designed for the elementary principal, the book provides a framework for calendar development plus a resource of sample documents to assist with communication.

Ricken, R., Terc, M., & Ayres, I. (2001). *The secondary school principal's calendar.* Thousand Oaks, CA: Corwin Press.

> Designed for the secondary principal, the book provides a framework for calendar development plus a resource of sample documents to assist with communication needs.

Straub, J. T. (2000). The rookie manager: A guide to surviving your first year in management. New York: Amacom.

> Although written for new managers in business, the book contains useful information and applications for beginning principals.

Torre, J. (1999). *Joe Torre's ground rules for winners.* New York: Hyperion.

> The manager of the New York Yankees shares his wisdom on universal concerns of leaders and managers. Especially noteworthy is his message on earning trust and respect and creating a cohesive unit out of a diverse group of individuals.

Whitaker, T. (1999). *Dealing with difficult teachers.* Larchmont, NY: Eye on Education.

> A former principal shares nonconfrontational strategies for dealing with teachers who are mediocre, uncooperative, and negative.

References

Blase, J., & Kirby, P. C. (1992). The power of praise—Strategy for effective principals. *NASSP Bulletin, 76*(528), 69–77.

Brinkman, R., & Kirschner, R. (1994). *Dealing with people you can't stand.* New York: McGraw-Hill.

Brock, B., & Grady, M. (1995). *Principals in transition: Tips for surviving succession.* Thousand Oaks, CA: Corwin Press.

Brock, B., & Grady, M. (2000). *Rekindling the flame.* Thousand Oaks, CA: Corwin Press.

Brock, B., & Grady, M. (2001). *From first-year to first-rate* (2nd ed.). Thousand Oaks, CA: Corwin Press

Brock, B., & Grady, M. (2002). *Avoiding burnout: A principal's guide to keeping the fire alive.* Thousand Oaks, CA: Corwin Press.

Brock, B. L., & Ponec, D. L. (1998). Principals and counselors: Creating effective elementary school counseling programs. *Educational Considerations, 26*(2), 33–37.

Bulach, C., Pickett, W., & Boothe, D. (1998). Mistakes educational leaders make. *ERIC Digest, 122,* 4–14.

Davis, S. H. (1997). Remaining secure in a precarious position. *NASSP Bulletin, 81*(592), 73–80.

Findley, B., & Findley, D. (1998). Gearing up for the opening of the school year: A checklist for principals. *NASSP Bulletin, 82*(599), 56–62.

Gmelch, W. H., & Torelli, J. A. (1994, May). The association of role conflict and ambiguity with administrator stress and burnout. *Journal of School Leadership, 4,* 341–357.

Grady, M. L. (1990). *Visionary leadership and school administration: The missing elements.* Aurora, CO: Mid-Continent Regional Educational Laboratory.

Grady, M. L. (2001). *124 high-impact letters for busy principals.* Thousand Oaks, CA: Corwin Press.

Grady, M. L., & LeSourd, S. J. (1990). Principals' attitudes toward visionary leadership. *The High School Journal, 73,* 103–107.

Hart, A. W. (1993). *Principal succession: Establishing leadership in schools.* Albany: State University of New York Press.

Herzberg, F. (1987). One more time: How do you motivate employees? *Harvard Business Review, 65,* 109–120.

Katz, N. H., & Lawyer, J. W. (1993). *Conflict resolution: Building bridges.* Thousand Oaks, CA: Corwin Press.

King, M., & Blumer, I. (2000). A good start. *Phi Delta Kappan, 81,* 356–360.

Macmillan, R. B. (1998). Approaches to leadership. *Educational Management & Administration: Journal of the British Educational Management and Administration Society, 26,* 173–184.

Maslow, A. (1954). *Motivation and personality.* New York: Harper & Row.

McGregor, D. (1960). *The human side of enterprise.* New York: McGraw-Hill.

Mindell, P. (1993). *Power reading.* Englewood Cliffs, NJ: Prentice Hall.

Osterman, K., & Sullivan, S. (1996). New principals in an urban bureaucracy. *Journal of School Leadership, 6,* 661–690.

Ponec, D. L., & Brock, B. L. (2000). Relationships among elementary school counselors and principals: A unique bond. *Professional School Counselor, 3,* 208–217.

Ramsey, R. D. (1999). How to say the right thing every time. Thousand Oaks, CA: Corwin Press.

Rooney, J. (1998) Survival skills for the new principal. *Educational Leadership, 58,* 77–78.

Schmidt, L. J., Kosmoski, G. J., & Pollack, D. R. (1998a). *Novice administrators: Personality and administrative style changes.* (ERIC Document Reproduction Service No. ED427387).

Schmidt, L. J., Kosmoski, G. J., & Pollack, D. R. (1998b). *Novice administrators: Psychological and physiological effects.* (ERIC Document Reproduction Service No. ED427386).

Schwinden, M. (1998). A principal's perspective on administrative relationships. *Jossey-Bass educational series: No. 10. New directions for school leadership* (pp. 34–42). San Francisco: Jossey-Bass.

Sigford, J. L. (1998). *Who said school administration would be fun?* Thousand Oaks, CA: Corwin Press.

Straub, J. T. (2000). *The rookie manager.* New York: American Management Association.

Torre, J. (1999). *Joe Torre's ground rules for winners.* New York: Hyperion.

Whitaker, T. (1999). *Dealing with difficult teachers.* Larchmont, NY: Eye on Education.

Zalman, C. C., & Bryant, M. T. (2002, April). *The Solomonic pathway: Critical incidents in the elementary school principalship.* Paper presented at the annual meeting of the American Educational Research Association, New Orleans, LA.

Index

**CORWIN
PRESS**

The Corwin Press logo—a raven striding across an open book—represents the happy
union of courage and learning. We are a professional-level publisher of books and
journals for K-12 educators, and we are committed to creating and providing resources
that embody these qualities. Corwin's motto is "Success for All Learners."